I0416692

Daddy's Bums

By

Eileen Shannon

© 2002 by Eileen Shannon. All rights reserved.

No part of this book may be reproduced,
stored in a retrieval system, or transmitted by any
means, electronic, mechanical, photocopying,
recording, or otherwise, without written
permission from the author.

ISBN: 1-4033-4812-X (e-book)
ISBN: 1-4033-4813-8 (Paperback)

This book is printed on acid free paper.

1stBooks—rev. 09/12/02

THE KEY

So very many years ago I left my prairie home.
The distant fields invited me and I began to roam.
I found a new life far away, Exciting for awhile.
I saw new places, met new friends and lived along their style.
But as this way of living settled down to every day,
I began to feel nostalgia for my home so far away.

Diesel trucks on highways roaring so my ears would ring,
Brought to my mind the tractor and the seeder in the spring.
And in the summer sun I saw on beaches where I lay,
The annual school picnic on another sunny day.
And on a train late, late at night I'd hear the great wheels turn.
Down in my heart twas threshing time and I was on the farm.

I recalled my happy childhood and the rolling hills of home,
The winter sleigh rides, northern lights, the frosty skating ponds.

I told a friend of mine one day what had come
over me.
He looked at me and on his face I saw deep
sympathy.
I know he said go back awhile, go back and you
will find,
It's not what lies back there you want it's what
has passed with time.

He said we all go through it once in our lives and
then,
We know that what is gone is gone and can't
come back again.
The old home on the prairies, the mountains, or
by the sea,
Is just a symbol in our hearts of things that used
to be.
We look ahead, We don't look back except to
smile and say.
"Those really were the good old days but they've
long gone away"

Away down deep within our hearts there lies a
golden key.
That opens many, many doors each doors a
memory.
Now that I know this secret how can I feel alone,
I know it's here that I belong, here is my heartmy
home.

And when I want to reminisce some old friend for to see,
I just reach down and from my heart produce the Golden Key

Written by
Evelyn Renyard
"nee Pearson"

PROLOGUE

The autumn is beautiful here in B.C. The leaves are turning from brilliant reds to dark purple, to orange and yellow and earthy brown. The breeze soft in the daytime turns cool at night, and the rainy season is almost upon us.

As I look from the window of Daddy's last home I can see a brave rose unfolding in his garden. This is B.C. warm enough even in the fall to allow the leaves to turn and the breeze to cool, and still making room for the rose to bloom. Today the roses bring memories to me. Memories of hope. The memories sooth the mind and make us young again. The hope is for the generations to come that our seed brought into these unruly times will blossom pure and straight, overcoming all of today's pessimisms and fears, with the pride and honour of the heritage our memories represent.

It is with this thought in mind that I begin to record what has been told to me and what I recall of one family, my family. I hope and sincerely pray that all the data I can gather will be sufficient to make interesting reading for you, my sisters and brothers and anyone else who reads it.

A family tree is only a record of branches of ancestry, and our story takes much more than branches to tell. At this writing I find it overwhelming to think that our family once compact on the prairies of Manitoba has branched across the length and breadth of this country. None of us made a great mark in society but in the simple elements, love, trust and togetherness, time and space are of no essence. We are a unit. So be it. In my humblest of hearts I dedicate this book to the memory of our dear Mother and Father.

CHAPTER ONE

SWEDEN - 1850 - 1905

Nels Pearson came from a very poor family of farmers. At the age of fourteen he was on his own, in the world of hard labour and very little pay. His first job was with a carriage maker where the food often consisted of little more than dry mouldy bread and the pay for one years work was one outfit of work cloths and a pair of boots.

He was born around 1850- a time in Sweden when the poor were poverty stricken and found it necessary to grub their meagre living from the wealthy landowners. There was little chance of advancement.

How long he worked as a carriage maker is unknown, or what he did for the next several years but he was a strong healthy young man, tall and Viking like of stature with an unbreakable faith and love of God.

It is said that while working for the carriage maker one evening he looked up at the big mansion and said to his fellow workers,"One day I will own a house like that", of course they just laughed.

In 1875 Nels met and married Maria Jenson of Copenhagen Denmark. Maria was an orphan who had been raised by her loving Aunt and

1

Uncle in Copenhagen. As a young girl she had gone to work on a large estate. There she learned to make butter and cheese and became a proficient maker of dairy products. Danish cheese, being a product known all over the world demanded perfection from anyone who undertook such work.

After Nels and Maria were married they managed to buy a small dairy in the sea coast town of Malmo in Sweden. With hard work and putting almost everything they made back into the business it thrived and soon they were shipping butter and cheese all over Europe.

In order that nothing should be wasted the aggressive young couple bought a Piggery as they were called at that time. The cream was skimmed off the milk for the butter and cheese and then the soured skim milk went to feed the pigs. The manure from the pigs went to fertilize the land, which in turn fed the cattle.

By this time the Pearsons were employing a fairly large staff, all of whom worked happily and were fed well and earned a suitable wage. Nels then bought an Inn and Livery and subsequently became an estate holder and town councillor who held the respect and admiration of the town.

During these years the family had multiplied. Nels and Maria had seven children, Martin, Ludwig, Ida, Alma, Hilma, Hilding and Lydia. Their home was a beautiful big brick mansion, which was run mostly by a staff of servants as Maria was still very active in the business.

Nels and Maria loved music, so at an early age the children started to take music lessons on an instrument of their choice. Hilma studied the piano and Lydia the mandolin. Hilding began his training on the violin at the age of ten. Over the years he became a beautiful violinist with a touch that mastered the emotions of his audience and a knowledge of the story behind every selection and its composer that he played. His instructors believed that he had the makings of a concert violinist.

Alma was never very well. From birth she was afflicted with a very bad heart.

She was never to be roused by strong emotions of any kind and her welfare was a constant concern to the whole family.

When Ida was five years old tragedy struck the family with an unspeakably cruel hand. She had been an angel at the Christmas concert the church had put on, and when she came home she ran into the kitchen to show her angel costume to one of the maids she was fond of. One of the staff had just put a tub of boiling lye water on the floor and little Ida fell into it. The Doctor came right away but there was nothing he could do. Ida died within hours.

The family was in shock and Maria was put to bed and could not even attend little Ida's funeral.

She did not seem to know anyone for weeks and the Doctor was worried that she may stay that way. But Maria was a strong lady and came out of it. However the loss of Ida lingered with her for the rest of her life.

With business flourishing and the family growing up Nels had become a very important man in the sea coast town of Malmo.

It was only natural that he was approached now and then by promoters looking for financial backing in business deals. But he was a shrewd self made man and made no commitments without first giving it a lot of thought.

But he was also a man who drove himself to the limit and demanded more sometimes then his body could give. As a result, just about the time of the turn of the century he became ill with congestion of the lungs. He drove himself on even when very sick and it was in this weakened condition that he was approached by a company of contractors who desired financial backing to build three large churches in and around Malmo. After much discussion he did back them, unknown to any of the family.

His condition was steadily getting worse and before long he was confined to his bed. The Doctor told Maria there was nothing more they could do for him and he would surely die.

It was the custom in Sweden to toll the church bell for the dying. The bell would toll the years of

4

his life at intervals until he passed on. The bells had begun to toll when an old Doctor friend of the family who had just returned from Europe came to the house and asked Maria if he could try one more thing. The Doctor then prepared a bath of warm water and mustard. They lifted Nels into it and after an hour he began to breathe a little easier. They would let him rest in bed for awhile and begin all over again. After a couple of days of this they could wrap him in a warm blanket and put him to bed to begin a miraculous recovery.

During his recuperation much was happening in his financial world. The promoters who had received backing from him had disappeared and the bankers were preparing to foreclose on his entire estate. Nels regained his strength to find his biggest battle before him.

Auctioneers moved into his home and businesses and sold everything they owned. He and Maria had to stand helplessly by and watch all their belongings go before their eyes. All those years of hard work went in a matter of days. There was little left for them to start over with when it was finished. It was the end of their life in Malmo.

But Nels had one more iron in the fire. This one was in a small city in Sweden called Horby. The tragic loss that Nels and Maria suffered took a toll on Maria's health and she was in need of a complete rest so she and the younger children went to her family in Copenhagen for awhile.

While there Hilding carried on his violin studies. He was inspired to a point by an old violin that hung on the wall in the parlour of his Uncle's home. It had belonged to a relative of his who had become a somewhat famous Danish violinist and Hilding was thrilled with the stories he was told about this ancestor.

While Maria and the children were in Copenhagen. Nels was very busy establishing a restaurant in Horby. His older daughters Hilma and Alma helped him in this operation and before long business was thriving. Because of Alma's heart condition she could only sit at the cash register for awhile until she tired.

By the time Maria and the younger children came from Copenhagen it was a promising business that required hard work and long hours.

Alma's condition gradually worsened and she found it increasingly hard to take part in the hard work. After a short time in the new business Nels began to think strongly of new horizons—the land of promise—America.

Alma's Doctors thought that perhaps the Doctors in America could help her. And so the family began to make plans to leave their homeland and make the long journey over the sea.

Hilma was to stay in Horby until the restaurant could be sold and then join the family in America.

When they were booked and ready to leave Alma had a bad turn and the Doctors said she was not able to make the long trip at that time. So it was decided that she would stay with Hilma and come when she could.

Hilding was fourteen when they arrived in New York in 1905. From there they traveled to Montana where Martin, who had gone on ahead, had staked a homestead. However the barren country was too lonely for Maria so they traveled on to Canada leaving Martin on the homestead in Montana.

They eventually took a homestead in a Swedish settlement in northern Manitoba called Alpine.

CHAPTER TWO

1926
NONA'S MEMORY'S

My earliest memories of Alpine begin on April 8, 1926. The day Mother and Hilding were married, I was seven year's old. The wedding took place at the home of Rev. and Mrs. Sandeen in Benito, in the afternoon. Seigfrid Munson, a neighbour in Alpine, was the best man, and while I cannot remember for sure, I think Mrs. Sandeen was Mothers attendant.

Following the ceremony Mrs. Sandeen served a lovely meal, after which we three set off for the farm in Alpine in a demo cart with two horses pulling it. I believe the distance was about twelve miles, it took a long time to get there. We arrived at the farm around suppertime and met Grandpa Pearson and Uncle Ludwig.

My first excitement was the cows; they were all waiting to be milked. This job Hilding and Ludwig looked after. There were six milk cows and I thought they were quite wonderful. Their names were Olga, Molly, Steena, Carrie, Rosa and Nellie, "good old Svenska names". I made up a little tune so I could sing their names to them.

These cows always walked in a straight line, one following the other, and this pattern never altered. Olga was the "Boss Lady" and kept the others in order, she had a bell around her neck and it really rang.

There were lots of cats in the barn but no dogs. The cats were very wild because no one ever paid any attention to them.

When the milking was completed it was put through the cream separator, and I was very fascinated with this machine, never having seen one before.

This was a very important source of income.

Grandpa Pearson looked after the washing of the separator after every use. I recall there were a lot of little round discs which hung on a contraption that looked like an enormous clothespin and these had to be dried very thoroughly.

I was a lonely child, having always been used to having children around to play with at Dunrea, so I had to find my own amusement and cannot recall that this was ever a great problem.

One outstanding memory is that of the phenomena of "echoes" that existed at the old farm. To this day I really do not understand echoes, but remember the excitement of shouting "hello" and having about six "hellos" return to you. Mother taught me a song called "Little Sir Echo" and I still remember it.

There was lots of exploring to do, and some very pretty places around the creek. Grandpa

Pearson was very patient and let me trail around with him on his walks. He used a walking stick, so I made myself one out of an old tree branch. They were very pleasant times, and even though Grandpa could not speak English, we seemed to develop a really close companionship.

Then came the day I had to go to school. There was a quarter of a mile to walk to catch the van. The vans were really quite efficient, with canvas sides which could be rolled up when the weather was hot or put down when it was raining. In the winter there was a little stove in the van and we children could toast our sandwiches on it.

Because of the quarter mile I had to walk to catch the van I was the proud possessor of a pair of knee high rubber boots, because when it rained the mud was beyond description. I carried my shoes and my lunch pail which was an old lard pail with a little handle on it. Upon reaching the mail box I put on my shoes and left the rubber boots upright under the mailbox. One day when the van dropped me off I saw at once that one of my boots were lying on its side and wondered why this should be as the other one was still upright. Anyway I sat down on the grass to put them on and much to my astonishment there was a gopher inside it. You can imagine the chaos of me trying to get my foot in the boot and the terrified gopher trying to get out. Anyway, we both survived and I got the mail out of the box "which was my job", and trudged on home through the mud.

There was lots of excitement the day Mothers furniture arrived. It had been stored someplace in Brandon all those years following my Fathers tragic death at twenty-nine years old. I had never seen the furniture, so everything was new to me. It had been shipped by train from Brandon to Durban. It took two hayracks to load it up and bring it to the farm. I remember Mother cried when it came, she was so glad to see it. All the things we all grew up with were there. The dining room suite, sewing machine, bedroom furniture, a couch and all her lovely china, ornaments and cut glass. Everyone in the house was excited that day. I think Mother was especially happy to see her sewing machine.

I also fondly remember the lovely wild bird species some of which rarely exist any more. The red winged blackbirds, the yellow breasted blackbirds, the barn swallows, and perhaps most of all the loons.

What a wonderful thing our memories can be. But its time to put mine away to be dragged out another day.

CHAPTER THREE

THE HOUSE

Mother was a school teacher who had come to Alpine to teach the school there.

The Alpine school was a two-room school that taught grades up to grade eight.

My Aunt May had come with her and she taught grades one to three while Mother taught four to eight. They had brought with them their younger sister Addie and Mother's small daughter Nona who was three at the time.

Mother and Aunt May both played the piano very well, however, they were no match for my Aunt Addie. She had a real talent and a remarkable ear for music. She had only had three years of music lessons but when she played, she seemed to make the whole piano sing. She was seventeen when she came to Alpine with her two older sisters to watch Nona while school was in. And when my father heard her play he wanted her to accompany him whenever he was asked to play anywhere. Mother and Aunt May could fill in if Aunt Addie was busy but he really preferred playing with Aunt Addie.

Daddy was a lonely man who lived with his father and brother on a farm. His mother had become ill a few years earlier and passed away.

Mother always said that Daddy fell in love with Nona before her. I suppose he thought that she was lonely too, as the only children that came to the school were older than she was. He would take her sleigh riding in the winter and one day he brought her a cat that she loved dearly.

After a few years Mother, my Aunts and Nona all left Alpine and went back to southern Manitoba.

But by then the dye was cast and Mother was getting ready to be married, much to my Grandparents dismay. It was not that they disliked my Father, they were worried about whether he could provide for them as well as they liked. Times were tough and getting worse all the time and Mother was used to a lot of things they knew Daddy could not provide. Mother had already gone through so much when she lost her first husband just before Nona was born.

And there was also Nona to consider. But I suppose nothing can stop a woman in love. However perhaps a look at the home she would be coming to would have put a little dint in her bliss. Now don't get me wrong that's just my guess as she never said anything like that to us.

Mother was never as fond of housework or cooking, as she was of putting on concerts or decorating for a party or sewing. She loved music and singing, and listening to Daddy play the violin.

Now speaking of that, Daddy played classical music. Mozart, Beethoven, and Bach. Leibstrum's "Dream of Love" was one of his favourites. He always told us that he was a violinist and not a fiddler. He said they were like two different instruments and while he enjoyed listening to a fiddler play he did not play their music.

Grandpa and Grandma Pearson had built a nice house on the farm just after they had come to Alpine but unfortunately it had burned down just after Grandma had died. So Grandpa and Uncle Ludwig had built another. Grandpa never wanted Daddy to do hard work with his hands as he still wanted him to carry on his violin studies and he was always afraid he would damage them. It was of course an impossible dream as times got harder.

By the time Mother and Nona arrived there the house stood in all its glory never having been painted inside or out.

Downstairs was one large room. On the far side were stairs leading up to two bedrooms and a short hallway. The bedrooms were papered with old funny papers, possibly as a form of insulation. Nona loved this as she could lie in bed and read them. Downstairs there was a trap door in the floor that lifted up to reveal a dug out cellar.

Mother made curtains and did some wallpapering whenever she could scrap up a few dollars for paper.

There were mice in between the walls and every once in awhile we could see one peeking out of a knothole. But Mothers biggest battle was with the bedbugs. I remember seeing them on the walls at night and Mother would hold the lamp up under them and they would drop in. Then in the morning when she cleaned the lamps all these shrivelled up little carcasses would come tumbling out. The old expression "don't let the bedbugs bite" was a real threat to us.

Mother did the best she could to combat this menace. There was no such thing as "Raid" in those days. But she had a small barrel like contraption with a pump on the end that she used to shoot out the most ungodly smelling stuff. I don't think it killed many bedbugs but I do know we all ran for cover when we saw it coming.

Now this all sounds very bad and it might be hard for anyone to believe, but to this day we have wonderful memories of Alpine, our home, our Grandpa and our wonderful Mother and Father. I believe the reason for that is because we had a great deal of love, a great deal of music and laughter, and never a hint of violence. Now in the end isn't that all children really need. We always knew we were safe in their love and protection.

CHAPTER FOUR

THE CHILDREN

Mother went to southern Manitoba to have her first child in eight years. My sister Mary Evelyn was born in Dunrea on August seventeenth nineteen twenty seven. She was a beautiful baby and although Daddy did not see her for several months after she was born, as they had to wait until she was old enough to travel, upon first sight of her he was hooked. He was sure she was the most beautiful child in the whole world.

He did not have long however to bask in her beauty as I came along a year and a half later. This time Mother went to a nursing home in the town of Benito close to the farm. They named me Eileen Shirley. A year later they had their first son, Wilford Edward "Buddy". Then a brief pause of three years and George Ronald came along. I guess by this time having babies was old hat to Mother as she had both my brothers right on the farm with the help of a neighbour lady and the old country Doctor "who came to late both times". I do not remember the day Ronnie was born but Buddy who had a much better memory then I always said he and I were sitting on the dog house when the Doctor arrived and he always thought that he brought the baby in his little black bag.

Uncle Ludwig went to live at Aunt Hilma's about then. I suppose our little house was getting too crowded.

Aunt Hilma had come to Canada in nineteen twelve. Aunt Alma was supposed to come with her but she had died of a heart attack about a year before and Aunt Hilma had sold the restaurant in Sweden and sent word to the family that she planned to come on the Titanic. I never knew why she took another ship. Maybe she just wasn't ready, but fortunately she did and arrived in America safely. She married Uncle Amill and they took a homestead about a mile from us. They had two sons a few years older then us. Both George and Iver, Aunt Hilma's son, loved to hear Daddy play the violin. They really wanted to learn to play. So Daddy was giving them lessons. Aunt Hilma had helped them get an old violin but they had to hide it in an old barn on their farm or leave it at our place as Uncle Amill did not go for music, he thought it was a waste of time. They became quite good at playing but Uncle Amill never knew.

Anyway Uncle Ludwig moved over there. Grandpa on the other hand said he would not move away from the kids.

He could never talk to us much as he never learned English, but we learned a little Swedish and he knew a few words in English and we all got along well. He would rock Evelyn and I on his knee and always called us his "lilla flikas" which meant little girls in Swedish. Then he would bounce Buddy on his knee and sing "Rea Rea Ronca and "Gubin Noah". Heaven knows what all that meant.

Winters were very cold in northern Manitoba and Daddy would never let us go downstairs until he had stocked up the fire in the stove and got the room nice and warm. We four would sit up at the top of the stairs and wait for him to carry us down. After what seemed like a long time he would say to Mother "do you think it's time to bring *dos* bums down" and Mother would laugh and say "You know they're just going to be in the way but we can't leave them up there", so up Daddy would come and carry us down one by one. Now we could climb down ourselves but we always wanted him to carry us. It was a little game we played every morning. Then Daddy would head for the barn and Mother would make breakfast. It always consisted of porridge and how I hated porridge. Evelyn did too, but the boys seemed to like it. Mother would fix it up with cream and brown sugar but I still hated it.

Mother was the stricter of our parents and I'll never forget how angry she was at Buddy and I one day. There was an older man in the district who had dropped in for a cup of coffee. Well

Buddy and I saw our chance to have a little fun and just maybe get little Ronnie into trouble. So we took him away outside. Ronnie being only a year and a half it took us quite some time to teach him to say "Mr Aleen is a son of a bitch" but we finally managed. We told him to just walk around the table chanting this message. I must say it was a complete surprise to us when Mother never even said a word to Ronnie but took right off after Buddy and I.

At our home nothing was ever mentioned about sex or anything along that line. When Daddy would borrow a bull or a stud to service our animals we were all kept in the house with the blinds pulled down. However, unknown to them their very good friends had a son who was not so sheltered and he would give us a blow by blow discription of the whole affair.

Evelyn and I would cringe ever time it was announced that we were going to their place for dinner of a Sunday as we knew we must be very careful not to get into any dark corners with their beloved son.

Summers were very hot in Manitoba and we spent a lot of our time outdoors.

Below our house ran a lovely little creek with large fir trees growing along the bank. The creek was nice and cool to wade in and it was one of our favourite spots. Along one side of the yard there were two long rows of flowering bushes, one of lilacs and the other of honeysuckles. Our Grandma Pearson had planted them years before we arrived. This was another place we liked to play.

Then there was the ice house; this was a dug out hole with a shed built on top of it. All winter when the ice in the lake nearby was frozen solid the men would cut big blocks of ice and bring them home to be stacked in the ice house. They layered these blocks of ice with sawdust. Then all summer it was a cool place to keep meat, cream, milk, and butter.

We loved to get in there and play along the walkway that was built around the hole. Daddy would get angry with us if we left the door open, as he was always afraid the ice would melt before the next winter.

Then there was the barn and we did have a time in there. In one corner Daddy had built a chicken roost. This was a marvellous place to pretend we were chickens. Neither Buddy or I wanted to get up on the high roost so we told little Ronnie that we were the small chickens and had to stay on the low roost but he was a big chicken so he must get up to the top roost. Of course he fell and got hurt. Need I go into the fact that Mother was again very angry with Buddy and I?

The roof of the barn was also a favourite place to play. Now because of past experiences we felt we had better not let Ronnie climb up there. But Buddy and Evelyn and I would sit up there for the longest time viewing our kingdom. Buddy and Evelyn would jump down onto the soft grass below but I never wanted to jump so Daddy would have to come and get me down. One day Buddy fell on an old rusty cow bell and cut his lip open. Mother put tape on it and Daddy got the horses ready and off they went to town to get it stitched up.

One blessing in our home was Mothers old sewing machine. We really should have built a monument to it. Flour came in cloth hundred pound bags with a big Robin Hood on the outside. These bags would be emptied into a bin and Mother would rip the bag open and put it away. When she had several bags they would be washed and boiled and scrubbed until there was no sign of Robin Hood left. Then Mother would make curtains, underwear and sometimes even sheets with the cloth.

Then came the boxes of old cloths from our family in southern Manitoba. Mother would take the dresses apart and wash and iron the material and make clothes for us. She would do the same with the coats and suits and make winter coats and jackets.

Daddy always said we were the best dressed kids in Alpine. He was always so proud of Mother. Now to sew was a real pleasure for

21

Mother. To cook and clean house was a real drag. And while she managed to do the basics she never really liked it. She would far rather be sewing or decorating something or putting on a concert somewhere.

Where our friends would come home from school to great smells of home made bread and pastries, we usually came home to the smell of something burning in the kitchen and we would find Mother busy translating the Swedish words of a hymn to English or writing a poem or something. But she did so many other wonderful things that we really didn't care. We would not have changed one thing about her.

CHAPTER FIVE

Fall was always a busy time on the farm. For weeks Daddy had been cutting the wheat and forming it into bundles. These bundles were called stokes. The stokes were then stood up in bunches of five. These bunches all stood in a row down the field so the hayracks could drive between the rows and pick them up. One of the neighbours owned the threshing machine. He would go from farm to farm threshing everyones grain. For this service he would receive a share of the grain.

When the threshing machine arrived at a farm it was accompanied by four or five hayracks, six or seven men and a lot of horses. They all had to be put up and fed for about three days depending on how much wheat there was to thresh.

It was a very exciting time for us children, but a lot of hard work for the adults.

However they were a very jolly bunch and were happy to sleep in the hayloft or a pile of straw or anywhere they could lay their bedrolls down.

Mother had a big job feeding them all as they ate like horses. First there was a big breakfast, and then lunch had to be brought out to the field. She also had to bring out coffee and cake around four as they always worked until dark.

Supper was ready about seven and she had a long table all set and ready when they came in. Grandpa would have a basin and water ready at the back door for them to wash and then they would all troop in. Mother always made sure that we had all eaten before so they could have the whole table. It was amazing to see bowl after bowl disappear. They seemed to sit and drink coffee for ages after they had eaten and Mother and Grandpa would patiently wait to clean up.

Early the next morning it would all start again. By the time they were finished Mother and Grandpa and Nona were exhausted.

Fall also brought the slaughtering of beef and pork for the winter. Daddy did not like to kill anything so one of the neighbours would come and do it for him. This was another time we were kept in the house with the blinds down as Mother said we did not have to know anything about that.

Mother and Daddy were not brought up on farms and were not very good at being farmers. They did so much better when they got into their own line of work.

When the meat was ready they hung the sides of beef in the ice house. Mother had learned to can beef from her lady friends and it was really good. You don't see anything like it now and that's a pity.

Grandpa would salt some of the pork in a brine they had used in Sweden. Then he would smoke the hams and bacon in a little smokehouse he had made behind the house. All this was done late in the fall so the meat in the ice house would freeze at night and stay frozen all winter.

One nice thing about fall on our farm was the beautiful harvest moon. It seemed to rise up from the trees at the back of the house like a huge orange coloured ball. When we were very young it frightened Buddy and I, it seemed to be coming right at us. But Mother sat out on the grass with us and watched it come up one night and we saw it really was a thing of beauty.

About that time in our lives all our fun and games were overshadowed by a real scare in our community that lasted for months. There was a certain religious "cult like" group who were being pressured into sending their children to school against their will. In retaliation they began to bomb our schools and church's for miles around. Daddy and all the men in the district would take turns guarding these places all night. Everyone was still afraid that these people would get a bomb in the school some how. Nona was the only one of us that was in school at that time and I know Mother did not like to send her but the school board wanted the kids in school. They didn't want these people to think they were scaring anyone. The truth of the matter was they were scaring everyone.

The long nights began for Mother and Grandpa worrying about Daddy out there at night. And also they had no idea what these people would do next. We were all nervous but children go to sleep at night. Mother and Grandpa would sit up drinking coffee most of the night. We heard rumours of them taking off their cloths and burning their homes. There seemed to be no end to their radical behaviour until one blessed day they all packed up and left our community for another province. We all breathed a big sigh of relief.

CHAPTER SIX

1933

Northern Manitoba is extremely cold in the winter. We loved getting up in the morning and looking at all the lovely patterns Jack Frost had left on the windows. The colder it got the more patterns there were to see. There were lovely looking castles and trees and all kinds of beautiful scenes.

Daddy would bank snow around the house in hopes of keeping it a little warmer. Of course there was no indoor plumbing and it was a long way to go to the outhouse so Mother fixed a corner of the upstairs hall with a curtain, into which she placed a big pail. Daddy built a square thing to put on top of this pail to make sitting on it a little more comfortable. And there you have it. All winter long that was our indoor toilet and we did not have to freeze going outside.

Once a month Daddy had to hitch up the team of horses to a sleigh and go to town for supplies. He always brought us home a nickel bag of candy. That was a big bag of candy in those days and we would look forward with great anticipation to his return from town. When we heard the sleigh coming into the yard we would be jumping up and down shouting "Daddy's

27

home, Daddy's home" One night he was very late and also very cold when he got home. We heard him telling Mother that he had got three miles out of town when he realized he had forgotten our candy. So he turned around and went back. He proved his love for us in so many ways even if he always called us his bums.

Christmas was a very exciting time in Alpine. There was always a big concert and dance at the hall and another concert at the church. I have often wondered since how come there wasn't a big fire as well. The men would put up a huge Christmas tree and it would be decorated with all kinds of lovely things, mostly made of paper. Having no electricity they put candles in little tin holders all over the tree. These candles would all be lit when we came in. There would be one man on either side of the tree holding a long pole with a metal cap on the top. If a candle was getting to close to the paper or branches they would put the cap over it to put it out.

Mother and Daddy always preformed at both concerts and as we got older we joined them. We all had good singing voices and they were always teaching us music and harmony at home.

Just before we went to bed on Christmas eve Grandpa and Daddy would pull the Christmas tree into the middle of the floor. Then Daddy would get out his violin and play an old Swedish piece called "Dancing around the Christmas tree" while we all leaped merrily around the tree. An old Swedish custom.

Christmas morning was especially great for us that year of 1933 as we all got store bought presents from Santa. The boys got teddy bears and Evelyn and I got dolls with lovely china faces. Evelyn carefully put hers up on the dresser when we went to bed but I took mine to bed with me. It fell out of bed some time during the night and cracked its face. I was heartbroken when I found it. Mother fixed it up as much as she could but it was never the same.

New years eve was spent at the church. There was a service first then a big lunch and singing until midnight. Then they would ring the bell and everyone would stand and sing an old Swedish new years hymn "Times Clock Is Striking The Hour" It was very impressive. Some would be singing it in English and others in Swedish.

One day in January Daddy had to go to town for supplies. It began to snow really heavy and soon the wind came up and it turned into a real blizzard. During a blizzard the wind blows from all directions and you can not see anything. Mother and Grandpa managed to get a rope tied from the barn to the house so when Daddy got home he could find his way to the house.

They were very worried. When he finally got home he told us that when he could no longer see at all he just sat down in the sleigh and tried to keep warm and let the horse take him home. They seemed to know their way to the barn even in that awful blizzard.

George and Iver always left their violin at our place, as Uncle Amill was never to know they were wasting their time with what he considered nonsense. So they would ski over and spend many winter evenings playing cards with Grandpa and practising their music with Daddy.

CHAPTER SEVEN

It was 1934 and times were getting very hard for every one. The crops were failing because of no rain, or a blight that came on the wheat called rust. Sometimes there would be swarms of grasshoppers so thick they looked like clouds coming in. When they left there was very little left in the fields. Wind and dust was also a big problem.

These years were called the dirty thirty's and believe me they were dirty. Men were out of work all over and had very little chance of finding any. They had no money and had to hop the trains and ride in boxcars to get somewhere in the hopes of finding a job. They were called hoboes and they moved from place to place without to much success.

The songs that were coming out were mostly about the hard times.

"May I sleep in your barn tonight mister" and "Hobo Pete" were some of the most popular ones. Although we lived off the beaten path and did not see to many of them I do remember that once in awhile a stranger would come to the door asking if there was any work he could do for a meal. Most of the time there was nothing they could do for us but Grandpa always got them to sit down on the steps and then he would bring out a plate of whatever we were having. Sometimes it wasn't very much but they were always grateful.

We were living on very little ourselves right then as there had been no crop and only one can of cream was going to market every week. So there was that and Grandpa's pension check which was only twenty dollars a month.

The cattle were finding it hard to find grass as everything was drying up so they gave very little milk.

One of our horses got sick and Daddy and Grandpa worked on it for days. I remember they did not want it to lie down so they made a sling for it and that kept it standing for awhile but they finally had to let it lie. There was no vet within miles and even if there had been I doubt there was money to pay him. A neighbour friend told Daddy the horse had sleeping sickness and really there was nothing that could be done for it. Daddy loved his horses and said he could not put him down so he went into the house and played his violin while his friend put the horse down.

Easter was coming and we truly expected the Easter bunny would come. In our minds this had nothing to do with Mother and Daddy or hard times or anything. This was between the Easter bunny and us and he was magic. This must have been very hard on Mother and Daddy. Nona got so fed up hearing about the Easter Bunny that she told Buddy that he drowned in the creek. Buddy of course did not believe her and went right on talking about what he would bring.

The Easter bunny did arrive that year and we all got Easter eggs and a big chocolate rabbit. We found out years later that Daddy's cousin in Winnipeg had sent out a big box of Easter goodies.

Now Buddy and Ronnie and I ate our rabbits that very day, But Evelyn carefully placed hers on the dresser so she could admire it for awhile. She left it there for days for all of us to look at and drool. Finally I could stand it no longer and I bit off its ear.

Boys in the district were beginning to come over to see Nona. She was just turning sixteen and really had turned into a nice looking girl. Nona's father had been French and she had inherited her thick dark brown wavy hair from him and her blue eyes from Mother. She had inherited her musical talent from both sides. Her Father had been a talented piano player and had played the piano in the movie theatres for a living before the pictures had sound. So at sixteen she was a good looking girl that all the boy's were beginning to notice.

Mother always invited her friends to stay for supper and they would help Nona with the dishes and then take her for a walk. Buddy and I could care less about where they went but Evelyn always wanted to go with them. Nona tried to get rid of her but Mother always said "take Evelyn with you". Maybe she thought there was safety in numbers.

One day Nona came home looking quite upset. She told Mother she believed she was pregnant. Well I want to tell you there was a big fuss in our house until finally they got the message that the boy had only kissed her.

We really had no sex education in those days and I want to tell you there was probably less in our house then anywhere. Mother and Daddy did not discuss that part of life at all. But after all Nona was sixteen so they should have told her something.

The bush at the back of our place had all kinds of chokecherry and Saskatoon trees in it and Mother would get us all out picking berries when they were ripe. She would can the Saskatoons and make syrup out of the chokecherries. I haven't tasted chokecherry syrup since we left Alpine but I remember how good it was on pancakes. I believe the berry we called Saskatoons is what they call blueberries now. But the blueberries in Alpine were on low bushes close to the ground and were as hard to pick as strawberries. We got our share of picking these berries too. There was always so much wild fruit and Mother wanted to take advantage of all of it.

I hated picking berries. Anyway Mother had us all out picking chokecherries one day and I was mad as a wet hen about having to be there. I yanked a big branch down in a temper and to my dismay there was a huge hornets nest on it. I was stung many times. Mother said she thought it was about ten or twelve stings and she was very worried. She covered the stings with mud and I was quite sick for a couple days but after awhile I felt better. It only made me hate picking berries all the more.

We also had a vegetable garden, but the land was so stony and dry it did not do well. But in the dirty thirties every little bit helped.

CHAPTER EIGHT

AUNT LYDIA

Sunday morning was always busy at our house. After all it took quite awhile to get a family of seven ready for church. Grandpa never went to church any more as he found it to hard to sit on those hard benches. Buddy tried to use that excuse but it didn't work. Buddy found it hard just sitting still that long, as did all of us. Fortunately we always sat right behind the Josephison family and Mrs Josephison always had a bag of her homemade peppermint candies with her and she would slip one back to us when we started to get restless.

The Swedish Lutheran church in Alpine was only a few miles from our farm.

It was set on a little hill with lovely big fir trees all around it. Our preacher at that time was very outspoken and had a habit of jumping off the platform and calling us all sinners. But Mother told us he was just trying to make sure we all got into heaven. After the service every one would stand around outside and visit for awhile.

One Sunday we saw Mother and Daddy talking to a very nice looking lady we had never seen before. Mother had told Evelyn to take Ronnie to the outhouse and Buddy and I were playing in the trees close by. When Evelyn came out with Ronnie this nice looking lady was waiting for her. She called Buddy and I over and introduced herself as our Aunt Lydia. We did not know that we had an Aunt Lydia as no one had ever mentioned her before. It seems she and Daddy had had some kind of falling out and had not spoken to each other for years. She and Uncle Adolf lived in Benito only a few miles away and I suppose they had come up to church to end their hostilities. Anyway from that day on they became a very important part of our lives. We were never told what happened to make them stay away so long.

As September drew closer Mother began to get Nona and Evelyn ready for school. Evelyn was seven and starting her first year and Nona was going into grade eight which would be her last year in Alpine school. So the first day of school she sent the two of them off having given Nona instructions to take care of Evelyn. When Nona got home she informed Mother that Evelyn needed no help, evidently she had punched a kid in the nose for taking her pencil.

Daddy had got an old Model T car which made it much easier to get to town for supplies and one day he came home with a radio. What a treat that was. Now in the evenings we could listen to programs like "Amos and Andy", "the Lux Theatre", "Fibber Magee and Molly" and many more. We loved "The Grand Opry" and tried to learn the songs they sang.

Grandpa always had a bag of peppermints in his room. That was the one thing he got for himself out of his pension. He also had a pop bellied stove in his room to keep himself warm and would get us to carry wood up to his room Then he would give us a peppermint. He never ran out of wood that's for sure.

Christmas that year was very lean. Mother made doll clothes for the dolls Evelyn and I had got the year before and stuffed animals for the boys. She made a nice satin bag out of an old dress for Nona's nightgowns. We always got a big parcel from our folk in southern Manitoba.

It was always about the same Grandma Ford would knit us all very colourful mitts. She would make a big Christmas cake, lots of cookies and a big bag of candy. We thought it was all just wonderful.

CHAPTER NINE

Summer of 1935 was hot and dry again. The wind blew the dust all over and the crops had very little chance of turning out any better then the last year. In those days there was no such thing as welfare, but there was something called relief. Relief consisted of one bag of flour, one bag of salt, one bag of sugar and a bag of beans. I know it helped a lot of people but Daddy refused to go on charity so we had to struggle on as best we could. I'm sure Mother and Daddy were worried sick about the future but we had a few chickens and milk and cream and with Grandpas pension we seemed to scrape by.

One summer's day a sudden thunderstorm came up. It didn't last long enough for the rain to soak into the parched dry ground. But it did kill the few turkeys we had. Mother had got a few turkey eggs from a neighbour and put them under one of the hens. She had been so pleased when they all hatched. They had got to be a nice size and I guess Mother was looking forward to a few turkey dinners. Anyway when the storm hit we all tried to get them into the barn but turkeys are a very stupid bird and they just ran all over with there mouths open until they drowned. This was a real tragedy for our family.

Mother always thought that a more experienced farmers wife would have done better but until she came to Alpine she had never lived on a farm. Her father owned three farms but they always lived in town where he had a butcher shop.

One of my uncles ran Grandpa Ford's farms and they were having just as much trouble in southern Manitoba as we were.

Mother also was a bit handicapped; she had broken her arm badly as a young girl. It had been broken right at the elbow and the Doctor that set it had put it on sort of backwards, her hand always faced out. But she had learned to do everything with it that way. She could sew and play the piano and do her house work. She only found things like kneading bread hard to do.

A Doctor had told her years after the accident that he could break it again and put it on right but it would be stiff and she would not be able to bend it. She decided to let well enough alone.

The school picnic was always a big event in Alpine. This year Nona had graduated from Alpine school and Mother was wondering where she could go to continue her schooling. Evelyn had passed to grade two and I knew I would be starting school in the fall. But regardless of all that we were looking forward to the school picnic.

The day finally came and off we went for a day of fun and relaxation. There were races and games for all ages and finally a big ball game.

In a shed at the side of the school they had set up several large ice cream makers. These were large wooden buckets with metal containers in the centre. Around the containers they packed the ice brought in from the icehouses of many farms. On top of the containers was a large handle. The ladies then mixed cream, eggs, vanilla and sugar. This was poured into the metal containers. Everyone had to take turns turning the handles until the ice cream was ready. It was really the best ice cream I have ever tasted.

One day late in the afternoon we heard a car coming up our road. It was blowing its horn all the way and I thought someone was sick or crazy. Mother got so excited she was crying and we soon found out it was her Mother and Father and Sister from Southern Manitoba. What a joyful reunion hugs, kisses and lots of tears of happiness. We were very happy to meet the Grandparents and Aunt we had never seen before.

There were several days of Picnics, music and fun but it all came to an end too soon and they had to go home. Only then did we learn that they were taking Nona with them to go to school in Dunrea. We were not too happy about that, as we knew it would be a long time before we would see her again.

Finally my big day came; I was going to school. Mother gave Evelyn the same instructions that she had given Nona the year before about how to take care of me and make sure I ate my lunch and all that stuff and off we went with our little lard pails with the wire handles. I was not impressed with this school business one bit and decided that was enough education for me. But Mother and Daddy talked me into trying again. I guess the next day was better as I continued to go.

I thought my teacher was so beautiful and she wore such nice dresses. The dress I liked best was navy blue with gold buttons and a pink hanky in the pocket. Maybe I liked school better because I was so impressed with my teacher's clothes. For whatever reason I'm sure Mother was glad that she did not have to argue with me any more.

Evelyn was a good student and always got better grades then me. This didn't bother me much as she got better grades then anyone else in school. Evelyn was also very musical and while we could all sing she was by far the best. Even at that young age she could hear the harmony and would try to sing it with us. Mother and Daddy would get us to sing with them sometimes and we sang at weddings and showers. They had one song they particularly liked us to sing, it was called "Somewhere A Bluebird Is Singing".

So the year passed quickly and before long it was summer again. Long lazy days with Mother busy making old clothes into new ones so we wouldn't look too ragged when we went back to school. This year she had to get Buddy ready as well.

CHAPTER TEN

The dirty thirties were taking their toll on everyone. Some families were just closing their doors and leaving their farms and just taking everything they could pack with them. Their plan was to try and get work in the cities. Then there were others like us, I suppose, who were to poor to even move. Daddy was trying to find a spot to dig a well as ours had gone dry. I remember hearing the cattle bawling around the water trough. I asked mother what was the matter with them and she said "they're thirsty poor things". The men would haul water from the lake a few miles away but it was hard to haul enough for the house and the animals.

Now in our district there was a man named George Brown who claimed to be able to tell you where to dig for water. He used a pronged branch from a certain kind of tree. He called it a water witch and he would walk all over the land holding the two ends in both hands with the long part sticking out ahead of him. When the stick turned down towards the ground he said that was where there was water and to dig the well there. Well Daddy was ready to try anything so with the help of Uncle Amill and Uncle Ludwig they began to dig. They dug and dug and dug and finally did find water. Then they had to crib it all up so it would not cave in and put a pump in it and cover it. It was a long job but we did have water although we had to be very careful not to use more than we had to, as no one wanted it to go dry and be out of water again.

Saturday night was bath night. Mother would put the big tub in the middle of the kitchen floor and fill it about half full with warm water. We always wanted to be first, as we all had to use the same water. Mother would pour a little more warm water in after each bath. Then after we had gone to bed they would have their baths. I'm sure she used fresh water for their baths. That same old tub washed our cloths with the help of a wash board. Mother had learned how to make soap from one of her friends. She used lye and ashes; my god it was awful but it was better then nothing I suppose.

That summer Daddy was also fixing up the outhouse. He was putting in another smaller seat for us. My we were going to be stylish, a two seater yet. Now I don't know why but any outhouse that had any class had a half moon cut out at the top of the door. Maybe it was for fresh air or light or something. There was no such thing as toilet paper. In all the outhouses of the day the old catalogue hung on a wire hanger for that purpose. Of course one had to scrunch it up a bit to make it softer.

The very best times were just after Christmas. If you were lucky enough to have had a box of Japanese oranges, the paper around the oranges made lovely toilet paper.

Fall was upon us again and we were getting ready to go back to school. Mother had managed to get us all new footwear by making a coat for a lady in the district. I was so jealous as the material was brand new and so pretty. It was green with black and white specks. However we all got boots and that was nice too.

One day on the way to school the horses got scared of something and ran away. The van was bouncing around something awful and as I was sitting right at the end by the door I fell out when the door burst open. I hit my knee on a stone and by the time we arrived at school it was very painful and swollen. The teacher took me over to the cottage she lived in so I could lie down until school was over and the van came back for us. I was in so much pain all day that when the van finally came back I had to be carried into it to go home. When I got home and mother saw my leg she called Daddy and we got into the old car and off we went to Benito to see the Doctor. He said it was badly sprained and gave me a pair of crutches and told me not to put any weight on it for a couple weeks. Then we went to Aunt Lydia's for supper. For some reason Aunt Lydia thought I should stay there so I would be closer to the Doctor in case it got worse and Mother agreed. So there I was for the next two weeks and I must say I was treated like royalty. I was installed in their extra bedroom and Uncle Adolf would carry me upstairs and down. They never had any children and seemed to like having me around. Every morning Uncle Adolf would get up first and go down and make coffee and bring Aunt Lydia and I a cup in bed. He showed me how the Swedes drink their coffee. You put a lump of sugar in your mouth and sipped the coffee through it. "Of course I would not know that because we were not allowed coffee at home"

Uncle Adolf was the janitor of the high school in Benito and every day when he came home he had a treat for me in his pocket. When I got feeling a little better he took me with him to the school and carried me up stairs and showed me all the rooms. It looked so big to me. I really enjoyed staying with them, but was very glad to get home again. Christmas was very slim again that year. Daddy's cousin in Winnipeg sent out a few things and we had the usual parcel from Dunrea. Mother made us a few little things. I'm sure we got better than a lot of children did that year. Daddy made Ronnie a little toy violin and Ronnie loved it. From then on, all that winter when George, Iver and Daddy played their violins he would get his little wooden violin and play with them.

Mother's day had come and mother taught us a song to sing at the church concert. She cut out cardboard squares and painted then with brightly coloured paint. Then she painted the letters on. Evelyn was to hold M O and I held T H, Buddy held E and Ronnie held R.

The song

M is for the million things she gave me.
O means only that she's growing old.
T is for the tears she shed to save me.
H is for her heart as pure gold.
E is for her eyes the love the love light shinning.
R means right and right she'll always be.
Put them together they spell mother
A word that means the world to me.

This was the first time we all preformed together. I don't know how great we were, but how could we have failed when our audience was made up of family and friends.

CHAPTER ELEVEN

We had a new Pastor in the church. He was younger and a lot quieter when giving his services then we had been used to. We all liked him a lot. Before he had been there very long he started a band for all the young folks in the church. He had been given a bunch of old instruments and let us have the one we wanted to learn on. Buddy already had an old guitar that someone had given us and Evelyn wanted a guitar as well. He gave me a mandolin and Ronnie an auto harp. Daddy liked my mandolin and showed me how the strings were the same as the violin so he could help me with it.

Funny none of us wanted to play the violin. Maybe that was because when we tried it we could not make it sound like it did when Daddy played it. Evelyn tried to learn it to please Daddy and did get so she could play a bit.

Anyway we did love to go and practise at the church. We would walk to the corner of our road and Albert Josephson would pick us up and take us the rest of the way.

We did have fun with our little band and when we got to know a few hymns we were allowed to play them at church. We really enjoyed it and did learn quite a bit about notes and things from the Pastor, all of which we could have learned from Mother and Daddy if we had paid attention. Children do learn better from someone outside the family I believe.

Our Pastors sister had come to Alpine with him. She was small and blond and very nice looking and cousin George fell for her like a ton of bricks. Before long wedding bells were ringing. The wedding was very small and held in the church with Ethel's brother performing the service.

George was working for a logging outfit and was away a lot. They bought a small farm close to Aunt Hilma and Uncle Amills. Ethel had a horse and buggy and while George was away she spent a lot of time visiting Aunt Hilma and Mother. She also spent a lot of time helping her brother at the church. I expect the days were long for her when George was away. She was very religious. To the point of being just a bit sickening.

The winter of 1936 was very cold and we seemed to be forever bringing in wood for Grandpa. Not that we minded as we always got a peppermint when we were finished. A bag of peppermints and some snuff was about all Grandpa got out of his check but that didn't seem to bother him a bit. Mother used to tell us we weren't really poor we just didn't have any money. That did not make us feel any better when we went to school with mashed potato sandwiches.

Grandpa used to make cottage cheese on the back of the stove. We thought it was great. He also would set a pan of milk on the back of the stove and when it got real sour and thick he would put cinnamon and sugar on it. He liked it but we were not to impressed.

One day in early spring we got the big news that George and Ethel were going to have a baby. Aunt Hilma was busy making baby clothes and Mother often went over to visit her. I never understood that friendship as Aunt Hilma never spoke English and Mother never learned Swedish but they seemed to be able to communicate with the odd word Mother knew in Swedish and the few words Aunt Hilma had learned in English, and a lot of sign language. Anyway they were very good friends. I don't know why Aunt Hilma never learned English. They always spoke Swedish at home but both the boys spoke English they had learned at school. Both Aunt Lydia and Uncle Adolf spoke fluent English. They were younger and both had studied English in school when they first came to Canada. But there we were, some of our family spoke only Swedish and some spoke only English and some spoke both.

When it came time to plant the fields again that spring Daddy had got fed up with the wheat crops. He had had so much trouble with them the last few years. He had been talking to someone in town who had suggested he try Alfalfa instead.

So he did. Some of his farmer friends thought he was nuts as wheat seemed to be the thing everyone planted but strangely it turned out not to bad. He was able to market it in the fall and things were a little better for awhile. That summer we had a little more rain and with the sun and a little rain everything grew a bit better even the garden and the wild berries.

When George and Ethel's baby was born they named him Edward George.

He was a cute little guy with blond hair and big blue eyes. One day when Eddy was about five months old Ethel came over to our place in her buggy. She said George was going to be away all weekend and asked me if I would like to come home with her for a couple of days. I thought this was great and off we went. The next afternoon she said she wanted to go over to the church that evening to a prayer meeting. I assumed that Eddy and I would go with her but that was not her plan. She asked me to watch Eddy until she got home.

So there I was knowing nothing about looking after a baby at nine years old in a little house in the bush alone. When it got dark I was real nervous. Eddy was fretting and I didn't know what to do for him. It got windy and the trees around the house were blowing all over. I was very frightened. I got Eddy into bed with me and sort of hid under the covers with him. When Ethel got home about midnight we had both gone to sleep and I guess she thought every thing went well. In the morning Ethel said I had done so well we would have to do it again. After breakfast she took me home.

That night I told Mother how scared I had been. She was surprised that Ethel would leave a baby with a nine year old. She promised me it would not happen again.

It wasn't long before Ethel was expecting again. This time she went home to her family to have the baby and never came back to Alpine. She and George had not been getting along to well Mother told us. She said that Ethel was very young and being alone in that little house when George was away a lot probable made her very unhappy.

After a few years George met and married a girl named Ester who became a wonderful wife to him and a friend of the whole family. They never had any children. Ester helped support and raise George's two boys, she also never criticized Ethel and agreed with Mother that it was to much for a young girl who was used to an easy way of life to find herself so isolated with one baby and expecting another. There was nothing easy about life in northern Manitoba in the dirty thirties.

CHAPTER TWELVE

1937 was almost over. Christmas had been very nice and New years was coming up. We had heard our parents and their friends talking a lot about a fellow they called Hitler who seemed to be making a big stir in Germany. It had never affected us much until New Years Eve. It sounded really scary when they talked about the possibility of war. However Mother told us not to worry about it too much. She said she hoped nothing would come of it. So as only children can do we put it completely out of our minds. We did notice though that Mother and Daddy wanted to listen to the news ever night regardless of what we wanted to listen to. When the news was over Daddy would shake his head and then say to Mother, "I guess we can let *dos* bums listen to Amos and Andy before bed". The Swedish people seemed to often use "d" instead of "Th" when speaking in English and while Daddy spoke fluent English if he was worried or upset he would slip back to the old ways.

The first time I fainted was at Aunt Hilma's. Mother said the food was likely to rich for me. Swedish people are great cooks but they used a lot of rich cream and Aunt Hilma would fry salt pork and then pour the grease from the pan over the potatoes. Then she would serve cake or pie with big globs of whipped cream on top. We loved going to her place to eat. Anyway that night they just took me home and I went to bed and was fine in the morning. After that every once in awhile I would faint. There seemed to be no reason for it and in every other way I was fine for a few years. Mother said at first that I would grow out of it. But I new she was worried about it.

Grandpa was not well all spring. He had got a cold in the winter and could not seem to shake it. Aunt Lydia came out to the farm one day and talked him into going home with her. He only stayed a week and came back. He said he missed the kids. We were all glad to see him as we missed him to. I really think Mother missed him the most. They had become very close.

Grandpa did not seem to be getting any better and finally he was in bed all the time. We would hear him singing a Swedish hymn in bed. I don't remember it all but it started with "Tucs furd Gud" I may have that wrong but Mother said the English words were "Thanks to God for my Redeemer"

One day Daddy went and got Aunt Hilma and Aunt Lydia. When he came home he took all us children over to a neighbours and told us to stay there until he came and got us. We did not know what was going on at home but I guess Mrs Carlson was aware as she kept us busy all day.

55

Her two children Dorothy and Herby were friends of ours. Mrs Carlson waxed her large living room and then gave us all wool socks to put on and told us to slide around the floor. She said we were polishing her floor for her. When we finally got home Mother told us that Grandpa had gone to heaven, or as the Aunts called it Val Halla.

That was the saddest day of our lives so far because Heaven or Val Halla or wherever, we just wanted him to come back. Funny he never said one word to us in English but we understood him and loved him with all our hearts.

Grandpa and Grandma Ford came from Dunrea and brought Nona. We were all very glad to see them but it was a very sad time. Grandpa had been well loved by everyone. It was a good thing Mothers friends kept bringing food over, as Mother was too upset to cook very much. In the years she had known Grandpa she had learned to love and depend on him in so many ways. His favourite hymn was sung at his funeral. It was one that Mother and Daddy had translated into English so again some were singing in Swedish and some in English. The hymn was called

Glory for Me

When all my trials and troubles are o'er
And I am safe on that beautiful shore.

Just to be near the dear Lord I adore.
Down thru the ages is Glory for me.
Oh that will be Glory for me
Glory for me.
Glory for me.
When by his grace I shall look on his face
That will be Glory be Glory for me.

After the funeral our house was a sad place to be. Grandpa and Grandma Ford and Nona had gone and Mother walked around looking so sad. Daddy did his usual thing. He sat in the living room and played his violin. Then one day Mother said "enough of this Hilding. Put away your violin, we are going to the lake for a picnic".

CHAPTER THIRTEEN

Things got very bad after Grandpa died. We no longer had his pension to fall back on. The summer of 1938 a big hail storm finished most of the crops in the district including ours. The hens had quit laying eggs so we ate them. We still had a little cream and milk. But there were only two cows left. Daddy tried to sell Watkins products but no one had any money so they paid him in eggs and chickens. This was all very needed stuff but it didn't pay for the products Daddy needed to go on, so that was a bust. One day Mother had made a bunch of potholders and doilies and small stuff and went walking door to door trying to sell them. She made enough for a pail of jam and some bread. That was what we had for supper.

One day I found Mother at the dinning room table taking apart an old dress to make over. I asked her who it was for and to my surprise she said it was for herself. It was a rust colour and looked very nice. Then she looked at me and said "I have to try and get a school to teach". I did not realize then what she was telling me, but I know now she was telling me we had to leave Alpine. Daddy was so depressed he spent most of the day playing his violin. This seemed so hard for us but I guess in a way we were lucky. After all Mother did have something to fall back on.

That was the summer of our Ford Grandparents fiftieth wedding anniversary. Uncle Ivan came up to Alpine to get us as Daddy had long since sold our old car. We had a very happy trip down south, as everything was so new to us. We had never been any further away from Alpine than the occasional trip to Benito. Little did we know when we got into his big car that we would not be coming back.

When we arrived at Grandpa and Grandma Fords we were greeted with open arms and lots of really great food which was a real treat for us as we had been going pretty short for quite awhile. The first morning we were there Grandma asked us if we wanted an orange or grapefruit for breakfast. Never having heard of grapefruit we all immediately said we would have grapefruit please. We thought with a name like grapefruit it must have something to do with grapes and we loved grapes. Well it was awful and we felt obliged to eat it since we had asked for it so we struggled through it but I for one have never eaten grapefruit since.

The next few days were very exciting for us, as we had never met all the relatives on Mothers side of the family. First we met our Aunt Addie. She arrived from Calgary where she was a secretary for the General Motors branch office there. She was so tiny and pretty and dressed so nice I fell in love with her on sight. Then Uncle

Ivan brought his family into town from their farm about four miles out. He and Aunt Ethel had three children. Harvey was the oldest and he seemed very grown up to us as he was eighteen. Then there was Russell, the same age as Evelyn, and Joan who was just inbetween Buddy and I. We had met Aunt May but had never met Uncle Lloyd and Lloyd Jr. Uncle Lloyd was a barber and they lived in a small town about ten miles away. Then there was Uncle Geordie and Aunt Hazel and their daughter Noreen. They had just moved into one of Grandpas farms and were living in two granaries while they built a house.

Grandma and Grandpas house was a large old house on three lots. In one lot they had a big garden and in another was Grandma's flower garden, with the house standing in the middle. They had caragana hedges and large trees all around the property. Grandpa was getting older but he kept the place up so nice. He cut the grass with a push lawn mower and clipped and tended the hedges and trees so it looked like a show place. Uncle Ivan took Buddy and Ronnie home with them as there were so many people sleeping at Grandmas.

The day of the anniversary was lovely and sunny and I'm sure everyone in town was there. It was a very exciting day and Mother really had a nice time seeing all her old friends. Grandma looked lovely and they were toasted so many times with apple juice that I'm sure if it were alcohol she'd have been quite tipsy.

The first people to settle on the site were Dunrea now stands was a man named Mr Dunlop, then came Mr Rae and my grandfather. The town is populated by mostly French families. There were two churches the Roman Catholic Church, which was by far the biggest, and the United Church. The French people seemed to have extremely large families. One family in town had fifteen children. That poor woman must have been pregnant most of her married life. I also heard she died young". No wonder".

Grandpa had owned the butcher shop until he retired and was very well liked in town. They told us he never let anyone go without meat during the depression. He would keep a bill of whatever they owed until they could pay.

One of the best things about being down for the anniversary was being with Nona again. She was so grown up and looked so pretty. She was seeing a young man named Angus McCloud and we thought he looked pretty sharp as well.

One day soon after the anniversary we found that Daddy was going back to Alpine to have a sale of all the things there that could not be brought down to Dunrea. We realized that we were homeless. Mother had applied for a teaching position at a school close by and was accepted. She had told the school board that she had to have a place for us to live so they had agreed to build a living quarters at the end of the school. Daddy had found a job at a place called Shilo. The government was building an army camp there. Shilo was about fifty miles from Dunrea so he would live in camp. He promised us he would come home for a weekend when he could. We moved into the school house the last week in August and Mother became our teacher when the school opened the first week in September. Her salary was fifty dollars a month with a place to live and all the coal and wood we needed.

The schoolhouse had two bedrooms a living room and a kitchen. It also had an attic that the men had put a good floor in, and a ladder going up to it. Mother fixed the attic real nice for the boys to sleep in. Then Mother took one bedroom and Evelyn and I had the other. There were two outhouses for the school children, one for the boys and the other for the girls. We had our own. There was a nice little well for water and they had dug a fireguard all around the property.

We were on the bald open prairie now and prairie fire could be very dangerous. We were so happy to be in our own place again that we felt like we had died and gone to heaven.

CHAPTER FOURTEEN

Right in front of the school stood the flagpole. Every morning just before we went into the school we all stood around the pole while the flag was raised. This was long before Canada had its own flag, so the flag was still the Union Jack. When classes were over the flag came down and was folded and put away. This was all very nice but Buddy soon found another use for the flagpole. He would grab the rope and jump off the school steps and swing all the way around the pole. Soon he had us all doing it and it really was a great swing. However as soon as Mother found out what we were up to she put a stop to it. But as long as we lived at Bellafield, whenever we found ourselves around that pole and no one was watching we would have a little swing.

The first day of school we met the other students. There were three Butcher children, Alfred, George and Mary. Their Father was the treasurer of the school board. Which in itself was amazing as he could hardly read and he told us he had only gone to grade three. But I don't suppose there was much money to count anyway. Then there was Clarence Carlson who was the same age as Buddy and very much like him. They became great friends. Then little Annette Staples came. She was an only child who lived very close to the school. At first that was all the students there were, but as time went by we had many more.

Mother taught all grades from one up to grade nine. At first the children were curious about what our living quarters looked like inside as they had never had a teacher living right at the school before. They would come to the window at lunchtime and be peeking in. Buddy thought he would solve that problem so he got a pail of water and threw it out at them. Mother did not think that was very funny so she made him apologize and ask them in to look around.

Sunday if it was possible we went to Dunrea to go to church with Grandma and Grandpa. Grandpa liked to give us all a nickel for the collection plate. Grandma always insisted that us girls wear a hat, which we hated, but Nona had given Evelyn and I some of her old hats and Mother always wanted us to wear them. One Sunday morning Evelyn accidentally on purpose forgot her hat at home. I told her I did not think it would work but she left it anyway. I was interested to find out if she got away with it, as I would very much like to try it myself. Well we soon did find out. Grandma rummaged around in her drawers until she came up with an old black hat and poor Evelyn had to wear it. We always remembered our hats when we went from then on. We found sitting through the services long and boring and Joan was a bit of a fidgeter at the best of times. I'm sure I was no better. So one awful Sunday just as the service was drawing to a close and everyone had stood up to repeat the Lords prayer Joan giggled. Well, I really believe she could have controlled herself at that point. But I was thinking how embarrassed she must be and to my horror I laughed right out loud. Before a moment passed we were both laughing and we couldn't stop. It was a good thing the service was over and we were close to the back of the church, so we could just get out the door. Mother and Aunt Ethel were very understanding and I'm sure they knew we meant no disrespect. I never knew weather Grandma heard us or not. I kind of think she didn't, as I'm sure she would not have been so understanding.

CHAPTER FIFTEEN

Although we had been listening to war talk for quite awhile it seemed like all of a sudden we were at war. Great Britain had declared war on Germany. We of course, as a colony of great Britain, were right in the middle of it and so many of our young men were rushing to the recruiting offices to join up. It seemed hard for us children to believe at first. I know it had been expected. After all Daddy had been working at building an army camp at Shilo for months.

Mother started right away to get us and everyone in the district working to support the war effort. She would put on whist drives and concerts and dances at the school on weekends and charge a small entrance fee. The money went to buy cigarettes, socks, candy and all kinds of little goodies. When we had a good supply of stuff we would make up as many boxes as we could. These boxes went to the Red Cross to be sent overseas. Mother was also knitting socks and sweaters and scarves, as were a lot of the women in the district. These all went into the boxes. I have no idea how many boxes were sent from our district, but I know there were a lot.

Nona was still going out with Angus MacCloud. He had planned to join the navy as his Father had been in the navy in the first world war and he and Johnnie, Angus's younger brother, had already joined the navy but there was'nt a navy recruiting office in Winnipeg. So instead he joined the Winnipeg Riffles.

Life went on for us pretty much as usual. Aunt Hazel and Uncle Geordie were on a farm that Grandpa had about a mile from the school. That summer had been very hot and Uncle Geordie had been working so hard in the fields and trying to get a house built before winter. One hot summer evening Uncle Ivan came over to tell Mother that Uncle Geordie had had a stroke and was very sick. Poor Aunt Hazel was looking after him, and the farm and little Noreen. It was very hard for her. Everyone tried to help as much as they could. But that was really the end of their farming days. Uncle Geordie did get better but always walked with a slight limp after that. They moved to a small town called Elgin and started a butcher shop there. About a mile from the school in the other direction stood a big old empty house. It had once belonged to a family named Clark and it was always called the haunted house. We had all heard the story about Mrs. Clark and how she had hung herself on the stairway. The house had stood empty for years and the farm had never even been sold so naturally we really believed it was haunted.

One day when Joan and Russell were over we decided to go up there and look around. We were not sure we would go in, as we were a bit scared. But when we got there we saw the door was open so in we went. We were very nervous as we went creeping around downstairs but we finally found the stairway. We were just getting up the courage to climb the stairs when we heard a long moan from above. Well all six of us took off like a shot pushing and shoving to get out the door. Then we ran as fast as we could to get back to the school. Daddy was home for the weekend and he and mother were just getting ready to have a cup of tea with Aunt Ethel and Uncle Ivan when we burst in the door all talking at once. We had hardly got started with our story when Mr. Carlson "Clarence's" father came in. He was laughing so hard he could hardly tell his story. He said he had bought the place for taxes and had put a bunch of chickens in the barn. He planned to sell eggs. He said he too was exploring and was upstairs when he heard us come in, so he thought he would give us a scare. He was on his way down to tell us that it was only him but we were already long gone.

Then he asked if some of us would like the job of cleaning the eggs for him if he gathered them every day and put them in the shed by the house. They were not going to live there as they had a farm down by the lake. Buddy and I jumped at the chance of a job so the next day after school we went up prepared to work. He must have had alot of hens as there were so many eggs, but we got them all cleaned and went home.

We worked very well for a few days and then Buddy threw an egg at me. Well of course I had to throw one back at him and before long eggs were flying back and forth. When there were no more eggs we went home. When mother heard about this she made us go back and clean up the mess and apologize. Buddy thought we really should have got paid for the eggs we had cleaned but Mother told him to forget about it.

One weekend when Daddy came home he brought us a little dog. We called her Patsy and she was so good. Mother fixed a little box for her in the school and she would sleep in there while classes were on, then when she heard Mother ring her desk bell she would jump up and beat us to the door. All the school children loved her as much as we did. Uncle Ivan brought us milk every weekend but sometimes we ran out so Mother bought a couple of goats. We loved them and played with them all the time. We would dress them up and take them for long walks. We named them Brownie and Snowball. The only thing we wouldn't do was drink their milk. We said it tasted weird. Mother said we would get used to it but we didn't. So Uncle Ivan kept right on bringing milk. The goat's milk was very rich and Mother used it for baking.

At our Christmas concert Mother charged twenty-five cents admission. This was unusual but no one minded as the money was for the overseas boxes. This was the first time we had preformed at Bellafield and everyone really enjoyed Mother and Daddy's music. Then we did a few war songs. "Bless em All, When der Furore Say's" and The Old Grey Mare is back were she used to be". Then the class put on a play and the evening ended with everyone singing "The White Cliff of Dover".

Our biggest thrill that year was Christmas morning. We all got store bought snowsuits. That was the fist time we had ever received clothes that were not made out of someone else's old clothes. And while Daddy said the clothes Mother made were nicer, we all loved getting store bought clothes.

Every once in awhile Uncle Lloyd and Aunt May would take Joan and Evelyn and I over to their place for a few days. Uncle Lloyd had a barber shop in Ninga a small town about fifteen miles away. One of the big treats for us there was Uncle Lloyds drink machine. He always let us take a pop out of it and we loved it. This sounds like nothing now but we very seldom had a pop and to us it was a big treat.

There was a big family living close to Aunt Mays and we got to know their girls and would go over there to play. Their daughter Enid was my age and I thought she had the most beautiful eyes. One day I told our cousin Lloyd Jr. that Enid's eyes were just like our cats. I really meant it as a compliment but Lloyd Jr. told her and she was insulted. She sent word to me that they had two chickens and a pig that looked just like me. I was really very hurt.

CHAPTER SIXTEEN

PELICAN LAKE

School was over for the summer and the school board had work to do around the place, so Mother rented a cabin at Pelican lake for us to spend the summer holidays. Pelican Lake is about thirteen miles long and two miles across. It has large points jutting out into the lake, and it was on Butchers point that we were going to. I suppose it was called Butchers point because the Butcher family had farmed on the hill above the lake for many years. To get to Butchers point, which was about five miles from the school, you had to go down a long winding hill with fences and old gates to get through.

Uncle Lloyd moved us down in his truck and Uncle Ivan brought Joan and Russell as they were going to spend the summer there with us. The cabin Mother had rented was large. It had a big kitchen and living room. The living room had a big old fireplace that we loved, as we had never lived in a place with a fireplace before. All around the cabin were the sleeping verandas.

We met the other campers right away and were very pleased to find that there were three children about our age, Archie, Alan and Gracie. We found they were overjoyed to find that there were six of us, as they had been anticipating a very boring summer.

The first night we were there the adults had a big bon fire on the beach to get acquainted. Everyone brought out wieners and buns and drinks. We soon found out it was best to wear bathing suits as we could be thrown in the lake at any time for any reason and sometimes for no reason at all. Daddy came down the first weekend we were there and he and some of the men built us a really great diving board. From then on we could be thrown off the end of the diving board for the same reasons as above.

Every evening at about nine we held court. Anyone of us could charge another for something they had done during the day. Russell was the judge and Alan the prosecuting attorney, unless of course they were being charged. Evelyn was the attorney for the defence. There really wasn't much for her to do because if you were charged it seemed you were always guilty. There was always a lot of yelling and arguing and at some point Alan would stand up and yell, "that's irrelevant and not pertaining to the case" and Evelyn would yell back "that is the case". In any event the accused was always found guilty. The sentence was always the same. You had to dive off the diving board at midnight.

Nona came down for the odd weekend. She loved to just paddle around in the water close to shore. She had never learned to swim, as she was afraid of the water. One evening she was paddling around in the water and got into a nest of bloodsuckers. This was really unusual and the only time we ever saw a bloodsucker. She was hysterical. Mother and some of the women from camp rubbed her legs with sand and finely got them all off. It was too bad it happened to her, as she would never go in the water again. She loved the beach and going for walks and the bon fires but you could never get her in the water.

One evening Evelyn and Nona walked up to Butchers to get some milk. On their way home a sudden thunderstorm came up. These storms could come up very fast and the lightning could be dangerous. Daddy was there at the time and went out to meet them. He said he saw them crawling under a fence when the lightning struck the top wire and told us he could see the lightning dance along the wire as they were getting under. They got home all right but were certainly frightened.

The Butchers lived at the top of the hill. They were a "hillbilly" kind of family. Mr. Butcher was thin as a rail while Mrs. Butcher was very fat. They reminded me of the nursery rhyme "Jack Sprat Could Eat no Fat, His Wife Could Eat no Lean". They had guns and were often target practising. One day Buddy and I were going over to Carlson's when a bullet flew over our heads.

We yelled at them so they wouldn't shoot again. They seemed to think it was funny and the only answer we got was, "just about got you eh."

There were skunks around the beach. We could see them scurrying under the old buildings. Gracie said she had heard some where that they could not spray you if you picked them up by the tail. So one evening we went in search of one and were lucky enough to find one. We chased it out to the point being very careful to stay far enough away so it could not spray us. Then we threw small sticks and sand at it until it got into the water and started to swim. We then got into an old boat and went after it. Gracie grabbed it by the tail and we found that sure enough it did not spray us. We were pleased to see that Buddy was out in the canoe so I got the boat close to the canoe and Gracie threw the skunk in with him. Buddy tipped the canoe so he and the skunk ended up in the water and he didn't get sprayed. So Gracie and I went and got it again and brought it into the campfire where all the adults were sitting peacefully talking. My there was a lot of screeching and yelling. Daddy wanted us to put it in the bushes but we were afraid to get sprayed so we threw it back in the water and ran before it could swim back in. Needless to say we both faced court that night.

There was an old rowboat on the beach for anyone to use so we would often go exploring the lake. We liked to row down to Ninette the town at the end of the lake. The trip was about three miles so we would take turns rowing. The first time we went the sky was overcast so we did not worry about getting a sunburn. Somehow we were under the impression that you could not get a sunburn if the sky was a bit cloudy. We were wrong. We all came home with a sunburn and spent a very uncomfortable night.

Our boat had a slow leak so we always carried a can along to bail out the water. Rules on the water were not nearly as strict as they are now. I don't remember any rules at all. We had never heard of life jackets. Our parents would just say "be careful and don't go too far". I guess they trusted us to be responsible. Big mistake. We would take off for the other side of the lake in that leaky old boat without giving it another thought. I shudder to think what might have happened. People are far more careful on the lakes now and that's a good thing.

One afternoon when we were just about to take off for the other side of the lake one of the Butcher boys came down to see us, so he got in the boat too. We had no idea he could not swim until we were half way over and he decided to tell us. Maybe he got a little nervous as the boat was leaking badly. Anyway he was in charge of bailing the water out and to our horror he accidentally threw the can out. Somehow we were able to retrieve it and got over to the other beach safely. Then after dumping out all the water in the bottom of the boat we noticed that a storm had washed up an old boat on the shore. We thought that if we could get it over to our side we could maybe fix it up. So after much discussion, we decided to tie it to the back of our boat and pull it over. However as soon as we got it into the water it began to sink again and we had quite a time getting the rope cut so our boat would not get dragged down with it. We were still close to shore so we could have swum in but then there was Alfred. Anyway we got back safely.

It was a wonderful summer for all of us and a break from thinking constantly about the war. We loved the evening campfires with all the singing and roasting wieners and marshmallows. All to soon it was over and we were on our way back to the school to start another term. We had hardly got home when Nona came to tell us that her and Angus were going to be married.

CHAPTER SEVENTEEN

We arrived back at the school a week before classes were to start. Everything looked real nice as they had painted and cleaned up both the schoolroom and our cottage. They hadn't however cut down all the rag weeds and after visiting Brownie and Snowball in the barn I came dancing out through these tall weeds singing "Somewhere Over the Rainbow", not knowing that Buddy was watching. I was certainly teased about that for awhile.

Angus was stationed at Portage la Prairie at the time. He was expecting to be shipped overseas very soon. Nona was planning a small wedding in Winnipeg were she was working. Angus's family lived there as well. The wedding was to be on September tenth. Of course we all wanted to go but Uncle Ivan could only take Mother so Aunt May who was a teacher too came and stayed with us and taught the school while Mother was away. Uncle Lloyd and Aunt May had moved on to one of Grandpa's farms about a mile from the school.

We were very disappointed about not being able to go to the wedding but Aunt May was always a lot of fun and she cheered us up. She would make biscuits and pass them around calling them the wedding cake. And at night she would play games with us. She was really good at charades and would have us all laughing so much we forgot about missing the wedding.

Nona and Angus rented a small apartment in Portage la Prairie. They were only in it for two months when Angus was shipped overseas. Nona came to us at the school heartbroken and pregnant after he was gone. She stayed for awhile and then moved in with Grandpa and Grandma where there was more room. Nona was not well with her pregnancy and lost the Baby in the fourth month. It was a real heartbreak for her, one of many that came to her in the next few years.

Meanwhile we all went on raising money by putting on concerts and holding raffles and having dances to make enough for the ever needed boxes for overseas. Everyone had a ration book now. Sugar was rationed as well as coffee, tea, flour, meat, butter and gas.

One of the songs we did at concerts was a big hit all over. Mother had made a lovely horses head with big eyes and long curly lashes. She made the rest of the horse in brown material with a long curly tail. Nona and I would get into this thing, and dance onto the stage while Evelyn all dressed up as a farmer with her guitar would prance around singing.

The old grey mare is back where she used to be.

Back where she used to be.
Back where she used to be.
The old grey mare is back where she used to be.
Many long years ago.
She may be old and lean.
But she don't need gasoline.
She flick's her tail at a Ford and a Pontiac
Sneers at a Cadillac acts like a jumping Jack
The old grey mare is back where she used to be
Many long years ago.

Uncle Ivan's oldest son Harvey joined the army. The day he came to the school to say goodbye was very sad. Nona was at the school that day and I remember how she cried. They were close to the same age and she had just said goodbye to Angus and lost her baby. Harvey kept telling her if he got to Italy he would send her a big orange.

Every once in a while the school board would meet at the school in the evening. Kenny Nicholson was the President, Tom Butcher was the Treasurer, and Charlie Staples was the Secretary. There was very little to hold a meeting for. It seemed to be more of a social event as they always seemed to end up in the cottage drinking coffee and eating cake.

Kenny was an old friend of Mothers and had gone to school with her and Aunt May. He would come and take us to town every Wednesday night and to Killarney on Saturday night to the movies. I know he was very fond of us children. And both Mother and Daddy were very fond of him. The only problem there was, he was always hugging and kissing Evelyn and I and sometimes it made us feel a little uncomfortable.

Christmas that year was a lot of fun. At the concert held at the school we had a great time teasing Evelyn. Willie Butcher had given her a big bottle of Ben Hur perfume. Well you can imagine how much teasing she got from that. Christmas morning Uncle Lloyd came to get us in the sleigh. He had braided the horses tails and manes and put bells in the braids. The women had heated big stones for our feet and then covered us all up with blankets. And off we went to Grandpa and Grandmas for Christmas dinner. It was very cold and all the trees were covered with hoer frost it was so beautiful. The bells on the horses ringing, the cold crisp air and everyone singing Christmas songs. How could anyone want a better memory.

CHAPTER EIGHTEEN

We had a new girl attending our school that year. Her name was Joy and she was eleven years old. Joy had never been to school before. I never knew just why but she did seem a bit challenged. I'm sorry to say we did tease her a lot, but Mother was always telling us we must leave her alone. Her family lived quite a few miles from the school and had to bring her every morning. They were an unfriendly looking bunch and never came to any of the school functions. Joy was a sickly child and Mother seemed worried about her. She kept her in school with her at lunch and recess.

One evening we walked over to Aunt Mays and we noticed that Mother and Aunt May had their heads together and seemed to be in deep conversation all evening. The next morning we found out Aunt May was to be our teacher for the day. Before long Kenny came and he and Mother left in his car. We asked Aunt May where they were going and she told us they were going to see Joys parents. Joy never came back to school. We found out from listening to the adults conversations that Mother had realized that Joy was pregnant at eleven years old. It seemed the man responsible was an uncle who lived there.

There was a lot of talk about reporting it to the police but no one knew what would happen to

Joy if it was reported. Things were certainly different in those days. Children's services were unknown way out in the country.

The family said they would send the Uncle away and that they would look after Joy. They did not do a very good job. It was found out later that she was never taken to a Doctor and when the baby came both Joy and her baby died. We all felt bad but Mother felt the worst I'm sure. She said she should have done more but they had assured her they would get her to a Doctor. The Uncle was never charged with anything. I really believe this would not happen today and it is very good that some things have changed for the better.

In the fall of each year we had a field day. All the schools around would dress in costumes and a big parade was held in the town of Killarney. The school with the best costumes would receive a prize. Mother decided to dress us all in Mexican costumes this year. Aunt May helped Mother make the costumes. They made dirndl skirts and white Mexican style tops for the girls and tight black pants with white shirts and very fancy vests for the boys. They bought nice shawls for us girls and big Mexican hats for the boys.

Now wouldn't you think we would get a prize? But we did not. The prize went to a school dressed as rabbits. We were sure we looked better but Mother said we must be good sports about it.

After the parade there were games and races and in the evening the ball games started between the different schools. We had each been given twenty five cents to buy candy and ice cream with. That doesn't seem like much spending money, but prices were much different then.

The families always brought a large picnic lunch. There would be fried chicken, boiled eggs and sandwiches and always a few of Aunt Ethel's pies. She was the best pie baker I have ever known. The men would park the cars in the shade of a big tree and blankets would be laid out for us to sit on. Then the women would lay a tablecloth on the ground and set out the food. After we had eaten, everything went back in the cars to come out again at supper time. Manitoba is very hot in the summer and there was no such thing as ice. I have wondered since how we never got sick with food poisoning. But we never did. Maybe that generation had stronger stomachs. When it was all over we went home played out and ready for bed.

We loved to watch Nona smoke, she looked so glamorous. Just like Betty Davis in the movies. We all wanted to try it, but of course there was no way we could get cigarettes. So one day Joan sneaked some of Uncle Ivan's pipe tobacco and we took off for the bush. We rolled the pipe tobacco in some paper and licked the sides to keep the tobacco in. We all got to feeling pretty sick and it tasted awful so we gave up smoking.

CHAPTER NINETEEN

Everyone was growing victory gardens, Aunt Ethel and Uncle Ivan's was huge. They always had a big garden but during the war years it was a lot bigger. They planted a quarter of an acre in potatoes alone and at least that much again in vegetables. We would go over to their place to help with the gardening as there was no place to plant a garden at the school. In the evening we would play games. Our favourite game was treasure hunt. The boys would hide a treasure and then draw a map to its location. It sometimes took us a long time to find the treasure as the map would have us going all over the farm. One day after a long search we found that they had put a snake in the box. This really made us mad, so when it was our turn we found a nice fresh cow pie and put it in a box for them. But most of the time we found something nicer to give each other.

The farmers were selling most or all of there cream to the dairies for overseas use and butter was on ration. But about that time a new product came out called margarine. It was a butter substitute and came in pound squares that looked like lard. On top of each pound was a little package of orange food colouring. To make it look like butter you had to mix this dye into the margarine. We were not used to this and did not like it much, but anything for the war effort. Saccharin came out about then also. It was a sugar substitute. Mother tried to make puddings and cake with it but it seemed to have a bitter taste and we were not impressed. Over the years both these substitutes have improved and are used all the time, but at that time they were new and not nearly as nice.

When summer holiday's came around Mother had to go to Summer school to renew her licence, so we were going to stay with family for the summer. Mostly at Uncle Ivan's as that's where we liked it best. The first week Evelyn went to Aunt May's to help her with some housecleaning. Aunt May had a book of Robert Services poems and Evelyn really loved them. When she came back she was forever quoting "Dangerous Dan MaGrau and The Cremation of Sam Magee".

Joan and I went to Grandmas for awhile. Now Grandma was a feisty Scotch lady and you never new what she would be up to next. One morning when we got up we found her painting the stair well. Now Grandma was nearly eighty and the stair well was really high. She had propped a ladder up against the wall on one side and had a barrel on the other and across this she had placed a long plank. And there she was prancing along this plank with her paint and brushes. We asked her to come down which only made matters worse as she began to bounce up and down to show us how safe it was. So we did the next best thing, we went and got Grandpa and he talked her into coming down with the promise that he would get one of the boys from town to come and paint it for her. Of course that meant he had to do this right away as she would be back up there if he didn't.

Grandpa was a small Irish gentleman. He was always telling us stories and taking us over to town for ice cream. He looked after the grounds to perfection and this was no small job. The house sat in the middle of half an acre. He had planted lovely hedges all around the property and every few days he would be out clipping them so they always looked nice. He cut that large lawn with a push lawn mower and watered it so that even in the hot prairie summers it was always nice and green.

He had bought a Ford car right out of the show window in Winnipeg years before and it was his pride and joy. It was kept in the garage at all times unless he was using it and he was always washing and waxing it and fussing with it. In a few days he took Joan and I back to the farm but all summer long if Aunt Ethel needed a break some of us would go into their place or to Aunt Mays.

Summer on the prairies are always very hot and the summer of 1941 was one of the hottest. Dust storms would come up suddenly and you had to run for the house as the dust was so thick it nearly choked you. It seemed to get into the house even with all the doors and windows shut. After the wind died down we had to wash and dust everything. However that was not as bad as the thunder storms. They could be vicious. Most of the houses and barns had a lightning rod on the roof, but we were always hearing about some ones house or barn being struck. One night we had a bad thunder storm and in the morning we found that the MacDonald's barn had been hit by lightning and burned to the ground. They were able to get all the animals out except for the children's two ponies. They had been at the far end of the barn and the family just couldn't get to them. We all felt so sorry for the MacDonald children. There was nothing you could say to them to make them feel any better. All the men in the district were over helping them clean it up and start to raise a new barn.

Jimmy and Blanch Morrison lived about two miles from Uncle Ivan's. They were a young couple with two small children. Jimmy's father lived with them also. He had had a stroke and was bedridden. We loved going over there as they were a real fun couple. One day they asked Evelyn to stay with them and help Blanch and she was only to glad to stay. She loved being there and was very fond of Jimmy's father. So she moved over there for the rest of the summer.

One very hot day the five of us were playing in the loft of the barn. Uncle Ivan had piled a bunch of hay on the ground just under the loft door and we were having a great time jumping from the loft into this pile of hay. We hadn't noticed that it was getting windy and the clouds were really starting to roll around. When we stopped to have a break we were sitting up in the loft door. We noticed how dark the clouds were and then we saw the funnel pop out of the clouds and race along near the ground over close to our school.

Aunt Ethel was yelling at us to get out of the barn and down to the root cellar. The wind was very strong and we all stayed in the root cellar for about an hour. Fortunately the twister did not come down near us but it did come down about fifteen miles away and did a lot of damage. Uncle Ivan took us over to the site were it hit a few day's later. It was a mess. Evelyn was with us and she found a piano key away off in a field. We saw pieces of straw sticking right into a tree. Houses and barns were down. We didn't stay long as it was too sad.

Aunt Ethel needed a few days rest so Uncle Lloyd came and got the boys and Joan and I went in to Grandmas for awhile. When we got to Grandmas she was cleaning the stove pipes. What a sight! She was up on the stove taking all the pipes apart. Grandpa was sitting at the table, as she had informed him she did not need any help. But evidently that did not mean Joan and I were off the hook. She had us carting all these pipes out to the back field and scraping and shaking all the soot out of them. Then we had to clean and polish them before she would allow them back in the house. "My God she was like an army General when she got going".

Sometimes I make her sound really bossy and she was, but she had a heart of gold.

The people in town would come and get her if someone was sick and old Doc Roy was not around. She would fix bad cuts and look after the sick. Baby's were her special love, and she would see them through anything that came along. The folks in town really loved her. She was real good with me as I was still having the odd fainting spell. I know this worried Mother as all the Doctors I had been to still could not figure out what caused them.

In a few day's we were all back at Uncle Ivan's. Harvey was home on leave so Aunt Ethel had fixed up a unused granary for him. We loved to tease him about his girl friend and play all sorts of little tricks on him. He had a way of getting even though. One day he gave Joan and I what he said was a chocolate bar, in reality it was a plug of chewing tobacco. Boy was it awful. One night when we went to bed we found our bed full of grass and stones. When we took the covers off to clean it up our bed cloths started going out the window and over the kitchen roof. We ran out side to try and catch them but by the time we got down stairs and outside Harvey had them in his granary with the door locked. That night we had to sleep without covers. Good thing it was warm. Aunt Ethel gave us no sympathy at all in the morning.

Nona and Ronnie - Just before she left Alpine

Cousin George and Grandpa, Evelyn and Eileen

Buddy, Evelyn and Eileen

Aunt Lydia and Uncle Adolf

Mother, Nona, Evelyn, Eileen and Buddy

**Nona and Daddy at Alpine School before
Mother and Daddy married**

Nona on the old farm

Daddy and Evelyn - 1928

Evelyn and Eileen

Eileen Shannon

Grandma Ford in her garden

Grandma and Grandpa Ford

Ford Grandchildren

**Grandma and Grandpa 50th Wedding
Anniversary**

From left Buddy, Russel, Ronnie, Lloyd Jr. 1937

Bellafield School on Field Day 1940

**Music in the field Evelyn,
Eileen, Ronnie, Buddy**

Evelyn at Shilo Army Camp 1942

CHAPTER TWENTY

The last week in August Mother was coming home. We were certainly looking forward to her return as we were ready to go back home. Uncle Ivan drove us down to the school on the day of her return. It was wonderful to have her back home again. She first wanted to thank Uncle Ivan and Aunt Ethel for helping her all summer. She insisted that Joan and Russell stay with us for a few days so Aunt Ethel could have a rest after a long and busy two months.

By this time we had somehow acquired two guitars, a mandolin and an old autoharp. So we spent our evenings sitting up on a pile of dirt that the men had left when they dug out the cellar, playing and singing to the old harvest moon.

Daddy came home once in awhile for a weekend, but not as often now as he was in charge of all the building at camp Shilo now. One weekend he told us how very busy they were at the camp as they were getting a complex ready to facilitate a bunch of German prisoners of war who would be arriving before winter. It was scary to think that German soldiers would be living so close to us.

That fall and winter we spent a lot of time at Aunt May and Uncle Lloyds. Uncle Lloyd was having a hard time on the farm. He had taken it over after Uncle Geordie left and like Daddy he was not used to farming and was not to good at it. I don't think the farm was up to much either at that time. No one seemed to make a go of it at that place.

Nona spent a lot of time in Winnipeg with Angus's Mother. All the men in that family were in the service except for the youngest boy who was still in school. Angus's brother Johnnie was in the Navy as was his father. Johnnie had blue eyes and blond curly hair and I thought he was the most handsome man alive. One day he was at Grandmas and while we were all out in the yard he came over to me and said "you really are getting to be pretty Eileen". I was so thrilled, I was sure I was in love. However he did not wait for me. He ran off and married a girl named Effie. I was heartbroken for about a week.

We were at the movies in Killarney one night. At that time they showed clips of the war news before the movie began. Well this particular night we saw two ships in the middle of the Atlantic. The caption read "Father and son meet at sea" and to our surprise there was Johnnie and his Father shaking hands across the water.

Things at home were going on as usual. By this time we were asked to play and sing for all the fund raising events so we were kept busy. Grandpa and Grandma would drive over to visit us at the school every week. Grandpas eyes were not as good as they should be so Mother always wanted one of us to go with them when they went home, as far as the bridge where they turned and the sun was no longer in his eyes. So one late afternoon when Nona was home Mother told her and I to go. We were hoping not to meet anyone as we were in such old clothes. Mother said get coats on as there was a cool wind, so Nona grabbed Evelyn's red coat, it was miles to big for her as Nona was short and Evelyn was tall, and I grabbed an old jacket of Buddy's and away we went.

On the way back home we decided to explore an old house that was just about falling down. You had to walk down a long overgrown drive and it seemed very spooky but we went on. We got in easy enough as the door was nearly falling off. Anyway, we were poking around downstairs for awhile and decided to try going upstairs. We had to climb up a very shaky old stairway that nearly went straight up but we made it to the second floor. We found we must be careful as the floor felt like it could give and send us falling downstairs again. Any little wind seemed to shake the whole place. We had just decided to get downstairs again when we heard a car coming down the drive. By this time we were both covered with dirt and cobwebs. As the car approached we heard loud voices and laughter and the whole building shook. I'm sure they ran into it. It seemed the car was full of boys from the district who were going to a dance in town. They had bought a case of beer and were going to have a few drinks before they went. We were too embarrassed to move, so we were shaking in our boots upstairs while they were having a party downstairs. Soon the language got a little rough and one of them said he needed to take a leak. Nona said "we can't let this go on, we have to go down". I said I would rather die but she insisted so we slowly began our decent. All of a sudden there was complete silence and there we were in all our glory. We said nothing, we just walked out and they said nothing. I believe they were stunned. One of the boys was going out with Evelyn sometimes. We found out later through Evelyn that they were just as embarrassed as we were. Anyway we walked in silence for about half a mile and then we sat down on the grass and laughed until we were in tears. We were still laughing when we got home and when we told Mother she was laughing. I think the only one who wasn't laughing was Evelyn. She said she could never look Gordon in the face again. However they were together again that same weekend. He told her that he really hated that red coat, it brought back too many memories. The boys thought we were nuts going up those stairs. They said the whole floor could have caved in and Mother agreed with them.

CHAPTER TWENTY ONE

Nona was staying at the school for a few months. She was very proud of Angus as she had just found out he had been made a Corporal. He was in England and she was always afraid he would be sent into action. One night late in the evening we heard a car drive in. Mother went to the door and found it was Uncle Ivan and to our great surprise Angus was with him. Well you can imagine the crying, laughing and hugging that went on.

He had not been able to tell anyone he was coming as it had all happened so fast. He was on his way to Truro Nova Scotia to train a bunch of English recruits and take them back to England in four months. He was only home for the weekend. Mother fixed up the attic room for them so they could have some privacy. By morning their plans were made. Nona had a small insurance policy that had been turned over to her after her Father died. It was for five hundred dollars so she was going to turn it in and go to Nova Scotia to be with Angus until he had to go back to England. So within a few days they were both gone. We had only seen him for one day as they had gone into Winnipeg to see his Mother. Nona was back on Sunday night to get ready to leave. She was so happy. They only had four months together but

I'm sure they enjoyed every minute of their time together. When she came back she was pregnant again but lost the baby in a few months. Mother blamed the stress of the war again.

Evelyn was going with a boy from the district named Russell. They would ride their bikes all over the country. This did not please the rest of us to much as Mother had only got us one bike to share between the four of us and she seemed to have it most of the time. But she was in love.

Mother had invited the young minister over for supper one night. That afternoon Buddy and I had been roaming around an old building and ran right into a skunk. We got sprayed real good. Buddy thought it would be a real joke just to say nothing and walk right into the house. Boy did we smell. Of course mother kicked us right out and brought a tub of water down to the barn and clean cloths. We had to take turns bathing and changing then we threw our dirty cloths into the water. I don't think the smell ever really left them. I guess they were finally thrown out.

Grandpa got very sick that winter. The family didn't know if he would recover. Aunt Addie came from Ontario and stayed for awhile. When she had to leave Aunt May and Mother took turns being with Grandpa. When Mother was there Aunt May would teach the school.

When Christmas came we all went to Uncle Ivan's for dinner as Grandpa was so sick we couldn't go there. Mother stayed in Dunrea with Grandpa and Grandma Christmas day. After supper Uncle Ivan took us all to the Ninnet skating rink. It was great fun for awhile but thenI fell while playing a game called crack the whip and in stead of cracking the whip I cracked my wrist. I went into the girls changing room and found it was really swelling. It was very painful. Joan and Evelyn came in and told me to just stay in the changing room and not to tell Uncle Ivan because he would want to take us home. However after I had sat there suffering for some time the door burst open and in came Uncle Ivan to see why I wasn't on the ice. He looked at it and decided it should be x-rayed. There was no hospital close by so he took me up to the T B Sanatorium. The Doctor there x-rayed it and said it was cracked and I had also torn the ligaments around the bone. We then went back and picked up the rest of the gang and went to Uncle Ivan's. I was in so much pain by then that Uncle Ivan took Aunt May in to stay at Grandmas and brought Mother home. As it turned out to everyone's surprise and pleasure Grandpa began to improve and soon was his old self again.

CHAPTER TWENTY TWO

Summer was upon us again and we were back at Pelican lake. Ronnie and Rennie Armstrong, Gracie's twin brother and sister, were down spending a few days at the lake. Rennie's husband was overseas and Ronnie was an air force pilot home on leave. Ronnie liked taking us out in the boat and seeing how far we could swim. He would take us about a quarter of a mile out and get us to swim back. This really scared Daddy when he was down one weekend, as he was there so seldom that he was not aware of how far we could swim. Daddy was always a little nervous of the water. I don't think he would have made much of a sailor. Mother said he would stand on the beach yelling at Ronnie to get those bum's back in the boat. Of course we couldn't hear him. I still think it was quite safe as the boat was always there. We would swim awhile and float awhile and before long we would be back on shore.

The fish just were not biting that year but the Butcher and Carlson boys were putting nets in the water and getting lots of nice fish. This was against the law so we would put our fishing poles in the boat to prove we were fishing and go out and raid their nets. The first time we came in with a nice load Mother and Aunt Ethel thought we

115

had caught them. We had a lovely supper of fresh fish that night. The next time however, when we came back with a nice load, the Butcher and Carlson boys were waiting for us on the beach. They told us they knew we were raiding there nets but we claimed we had caught the fish with our poles. They said that was impossible. So we told them if they were so sure to call the game warden. Of course we knew they couldn't do that. Anyway Mother and Aunt Ethel said that it was not nice to steal their fish and we were not to do it again. We argued a bit as it didn't seem like stealing to us but in the end we decided to lay off their fish.

September was upon us again and we were going back to school. Evelyn was going to Killarney to take grade ten. She would board there all week and be home for the weekends. I was fainting more and more it seemed that fall and Mother had taken me to all the Doctors close by and every one came up with a different answer to the problem. But nothing was working. One Doctor even mentioned epilepsy which scared me to death but Mother said she knew how epilepsy acted and it certainly wasn't that. Aunt Hazel thought her Doctor was really good so Nona took me to Elgin where Uncle Geordie and Aunt Hazel lived and we saw him. He first asked me to go behind a curtain and disrobe. Well I didn't know what disrobe meant so I went behind the curtain and sat there. Luckily the phone in the other room rang and he had to go and answer it so Nona could run over and explain what I was supposed to do. I didn't want to but Nona said I better, so I did. That time I fainted right in his office. He gave my condition another fancy name and I went home with another bunch of pills and nothing happened.

About that time Aunt Ethel came down with some kind of ailment. She was so stiff she could hardly get out of bed. Uncle Ivan had to build a bar so she could pull herself up. She was also getting no help from our local Doctors. Finally they heard of a fellow in Brandon they called a quack as he was not a Doctor but had studied medicine. People were saying he was doing great things with these odd ball cases. So Aunt Ethel went in to see him. I don't know how long she was there but when she came back she was fine. One night Uncle Ivan came down to the school to talk to Mother. I remember hearing him say "well Ted what have you got to lose, at least go and talk to him" So in a few days we were off to Brandon to see this quack. After examining me he told Mother that he knew exactly what was wrong with me. He said that at the time I was born they were still using what they called baby bands. Baby bands were a long strip of cloth that was wrapped around a new born baby's stomach. He said that the first one that was put on me was to tight and had moved organs around. He said as I got older and began to develop it cut off vital circulation. He said he could fix this problem but it would take about a month of treatment and I would have to be right in bed. He had a house in town that he used for treatment and it was run by a very nice nurse. Mr Forester, he would not let us call him Doctor, wanted me to go there and he would begin treatments right away. So I was installed there that day and Mother had to go back and teach school.

Anyway Daddy came in every night from Shilo to see me. He would sit with me after each treatment for an hour as I was to lie perfectly still for at least an hour after being treated. The treatments were not painful. Mr Forester would sort of massage my stomach and push things around. It was a long lonely month and I was so sick of being in bed. I was also homesick But the nurse and her staff were really nice and soon it was over and Uncle Ivan and Mother came in to get me. I was so glad to be going home. Anyway quack or not I never fainted again and that was a big blessing.

Years later I was visiting Joan in Brandon and she showed me a huge hospital on the hill out side of town. She said "I bet you don't know what that is". Then she told me that it was Mr Foresters clinic of alternative medicine. A far cry from the little house with one nurse that I went to.

One day after school little Annette Staples was not feeling well so I walked her home from school. When we got to her place her Mother wanted to thank me so she went out to the hen house and brought me in a nice little red hen. I thought she was so cute I wanted to make a pet of her. Mother said it simply could not live alone in the barn as it was getting pretty cold. Anyway she said she was sure it was intended to be our supper so she would get someone to kill it. But I was sure I could keep it warm enough. I put a blanket in a box and put her in it. Mother said that I simply could not keep a hen in a box.

But being a little pigheaded I was sure I could.

The next day Nona and I went over to help Aunt May as she had fallen on the cellar stairs. She had been papering the living room so Nona and I decided to finish it for her. We had a great time teasing her about all the mess we were making of her paper and poor Aunt May could not get out of bed to see what we were doing, but really it turned out pretty good. The next day we went home and I found to my horror that Uncle Lloyd had gone over and killed my little red hen and they had eaten it for supper. I was not impressed.

Daddy came home from Shilo one weekend in an awful dither. He took a tub of water out to the barn to bath. Mother thought it was too cold to bath out there, but he insisted. It seemed he had got body lice in camp. He had with him awful smelling hair soap and about three cans of louse powder. When he had bathed and put on clean cloths he brought a tub of water in and was boiling his cloths. We thought it was hilarious and kept teasing him about the little bugs. He just looked at us and said "That's not funny you bums". But after he was all cleaned up he had to laugh too.

Mother had got us an old accordion and we were having fun getting used to it. The key board is the same as the piano and we were used to that, it was just the bass we found hard. One day we were asked to play the music for a dance at a school near by. We were very pleased because we were getting paid and the boys and I were busy deciding what we would get with our money. Well we played our hearts out and even sang a few songs as we were doing our best for our first earned money.

At lunch break we noticed Evelyn over talking to the folks that had put on the dance. We began to worry. Anyway we did not have time to get to worried as the announcement was soon made that the Pearson family were going to donate their music to the war effort. So much for that, we never had any money anyway.

Summer holidays were upon us again and we were back at the lake. Italy had been invaded by the allied troops. Nona was a mess. She was so sure Angus would be there she would wake up screaming in the night and all we could do was sit with her and talk until she could go back to sleep. As soon as he could Angus let her know that he was still in England.

But Harvey wasn't in England he was in Italy. Aunt Ethel and Uncle Ivan were so worried the whole family felt for them and hoped to hear news of him soon. No one can know what a worry it is when a family member is in active duty. Only the people who have been through it can know.

The camp fires at the lake were still lit every night but it was a much quieter bunch that gathered around them. Everyone there had someone over seas. The songs that were sung were all war songs. I will always remember those songs and the sad look on the faces around the fire. The last song we sang before leaving for the night was always,"When the lights go on again, all over the world"

CHAPTER TWENTY THREE

German prisoners of war were arriving at Shilo. Rather scary stuff for us as we were sort of under the impression that German soldiers were all next thing to monsters. However, after they had been there a week or so Daddy told us he felt sorry for them. He said most of them were just boys. He said they were in a strange land and couldn't even speak the language. But there were some similarities between German and Swedish and he could understand a little of what they said and I guess they could understand some of what Daddy said. He was talking to the officers to see if he could get them out working on the roads to give them something to do. He finely did get them some jobs, as he said where could go anyway. He told us that from what he could understand they liked being in Canada and were sorry they would be sent back after the war. One of the men from Germany had worked on the Bismarck when it was being built. In his spare time he was carving a duplicate ship of the Bismarck and making a lovely job of it. When the war was over he gave it to Daddy with a card of thanks. Daddy had it put under glass and it sat in our house from then on.

Christmas dinner that year was held at the school as it was getting to be to much for

Grandma to have everyone there. Daddy fixed long tables in the school room and everyone brought their own special dish. Someone had brought stuffed olives. We had never tasted them before but most of the adults loved them. Uncle Ivan told us that if we ate three of them we would develop a taste for them so we struggled through three and still thought they were awful. So much for olives.

Daddy got to telling us how silly the new dances were. He had seen a lot of them in the officers mess. The new dance he decided to demonstrate was called the jitter bug. Everyone in the family was laughing their heads off by the time he got through. As time went by we all got very fond of the jitter bug dance. All that is except Daddy.

Late New years eve we had just gone to bed when we heard some noises in the school. Daddy was still home so he and Mother went in to see what was going on. They found Teddy Armstrong and Sam Black and their girlfriends, all from the district, in there. They had been trying to go to a dance in Killarney and got stuck in the snow. It was very cold out and they had walked back to the school. The girls were in high heeled shoes and silk stockings and the boys had on dress shoes. They were in bad shape. There feet were frozen. Mother said they really should see a Doctor but that was not possible so she got their shoes off and began to rub their feet. It was morning before they began to feel better. We made coffee and sandwiches and tried to make them as comfortable as possible. In the morning Mother got Uncle Lloyd to take them home in his sleigh. The girls were quite sick but I guess they got over it without any lasting damage. Daddy said they were darn fools to go out in that weather without the proper clothes but I guess by that time they knew that.

The country schools were having a very hard time staying open as teachers were hard to get due to the war. So many of the teachers were in the service. As a result, alot of the grade eleven and twelve students were allowed to teach for a year in a country school. Evelyn was given a school north of Winnipeg. She was boarding with a Swedish family and the first time she came home was at Christmas holidays. She was telling us about some of the food they ate.

First there was "calves joy". This was made from the first milk of a cow just after she had had a calf. And "blood pancakes", made with the blood from a pig. She asked Daddy about these dishes as we had lived in a Swedish district and never heard of them. He told her these were dishes that the peasants used. I was a little ticked off at him as it sounded prejudiced but he was quick to tell us that the word peasant in Sweden was the same as farmer in Canada.

Aunt Hilma and Mother were always writing to each other. Mother in English and Aunt Hilma in Swedish. They seemed to understand each others letters though. If Mother got stuck on some words she could ask Daddy and I suppose Aunt Hilma could do the same thing on her end.

CHAPTER TWENTY FOUR

By this time everyone knew that the allied forces were going to invade Europe but no one knew when. In one of my letters to Angus I had said I hoped the invasion would never come. When he wrote back he said the invasion had to come, it was the only way they could get home. That was the last letter I ever got from him. We were always short of things like sugar and butter, tea, and coffee. Half way through the month we were using saccharin and margarine again. We were really sick of rations but consoled ourselves with the knowledge that the good stuff was going overseas to feed our soldiers. We were also being told that the people in England and many other countries were having it a lot harder than us.

The hall in Killarney was the biggest one around so Mother and a group of ladies she worked with were having a concert and dance to raise money for their parcels for the Red Cross. And we were to do a few numbers. Daddy was coming home for that weekend so Mother and Daddy would be doing some of their music as well. They were charging fifty cents admission, so we felt we must give it our best. Aunt May was helping us with our numbers and one piece was driving Buddy, Ronnie and I crazy. We were to sit on the floor in the back of the stage dressed in men's suits clapping our hands and singing over and over "oh oh oh mama", while Evelyn strolled on stage dressed in a pink long dress with frills all the way to the floor and buttoned up shoes, all of which Aunt May had found in an old trunk she had, and proceed to sing:

Gona dance with a dolly with a hole in her stocking,
While her knees keep a knocking and her toes keep a rocking.
Gona dance with a dolly with a hole in her stocking,
Gona dance by the light of the moon.

Well we got on stage and Evelyn I guess did not think we were putting enough effort into our part. She was amazing. She would be smiling sweetly to the crowd and then turn and give us a dirty look. Somehow she could do this so that only us three could see it. It must have sounded alright as we did get an encore for that one. Mother and Daddy played "There'll be bluebirds over the white cliffs of Dover". Daddy's violin was so sweet and beautiful that most of the women and maybe a few men had tears in their eyes.

Then they played "I'll be seeing you" and Evelyn sang it with them. They were called back twice. Evelyn had a beautiful voice, high C was nothing for her to reach. She also had a true ear. She could hear all the different harmonies while we were singing together and had no qualms about correcting us if we went wrong.

One night while walking home from Aunt Mays our little dog "Patsy" was hit by a car and killed. We were heartsick. The driver of the car came home with us. He really felt bad but he said he just never saw her. We had a little service for her the next day with all the school kids and buried her down by some trees in the corner of the school yard. We all missed her so much. I guess Aunt May knew how badly we were all feeling the next day, as she sent Uncle Lloyd over to get us. She said she felt like a picnic. We were amazed and wanted to know how we could do that in the middle of winter. She said we just had to dress warm. She had made a big pot of beef stew and another of baked beans and a lot of fresh buns. So we all got into the sleigh and drove away out in the field. Uncle Lloyd had brought dry wood and kindling and after the boys had cleared a spot in the snow he light a fire. We played games in the snow and had a great time. Then Mother and Aunt May put the pots on the fire and soon we had lunch. On the way home Aunt May said "Now who said you can't have a picnic in the middle of winter".

Spring came and Mother and Aunt May were going to put on a play for a change. Nona was home for the weekend so they gave her a part. Nona hated to get up in front of an audience so they only gave her one line, "I come to pour oil on the troubled water". Well she got all flustered and was pouring everything on everything. Mother and Aunt May just laughed and said she probably wouldn't make it in Hollywood. Anyway it was fun.

June sixth 1945. As soon as we turned on the radio we knew. The allied forces were invading France. We kept hearing the adults saying they hoped it would not be another Deiepp. Mother said we should all pray for our boys over there. This time there was no way Angus would not be there. None of the school kids came to school that day so we all went to Uncle Ivan's, as he was one of the few people with a phone. Mother wanted to contact Nona. We found Nona was taking it as good as she could and was getting ready to go to work. Mother was very proud of her and said we would all do the same, that tomorrow there would be school as usual.

We began working even harder raising money to send to the red cross. Several weeks went by before late one day Uncle Ivan came to take us to Grandma and Grandpas. We knew there had to be news of Angus. When we got there Nona was there and told us she had received a telegram that morning. Angus was missing in action. There seemed to be nothing we could say to her but she was trying so hard to be brave. She said there really isn't anything to say. You're all here and that says it all. Nona came home with us that night. She seemed to want to sleep with Mother. She stayed with us from then on until the war was over. We all tried to keep her busy and into things but she was very sad all the time. She smoked like a smoke stack and Mother worried about that. When it got real bad Mother took her to old Doc Best in Killarney but he said to let her smoke it was likely the only thing that was keeping her going. Months went by with no word of Angus.

Every once in awhile someone would tell us they had heard from someone over there that claimed to have seen Angus in a prison camp. We would get all excited and start planning what we could send to him when we found out where he was. But that word never came.

Daddy's Bums

CHAPTER TWENTY FIVE

We tried to go on as usual hoping and praying we would get good news of Angus. At least Aunt Ethel new where Harvey was and heard from him whenever he could write. And for that everyone was truly thankful. Nona on the other hand was a mess. She cut her hair short and never curled it. We had to talk her into eating, and she still wanted to sleep with Mother. Sometimes she was a little better. Usually that was when she thought he was in a prisoner of war camp.

The boys were away at Uncle Ivan's one weekend helping them to dig up the potatoes. So Nona said she wanted to sleep with me for a change. Mother wasn't feeling well. So we went up to the boys bed in the attic. At the time I was a little confused about sex and I was telling her that anything I had heard about it I found disgusting. Its sometimes good to have a big sister especially in those days and with parents like ours who just did not discuss anything like that. Anyway I got my sex education from her that night and she made it sound like an act of love instead of something dirty. She said you had to be really ready and truly in love with your partner and then you would want to be as close as you could be to him.

Months went by and no word of Angus. Then one day the wire came. Angus was dead. A letter came a few weeks later from a Colonel C. L. Laurin. He said that Angus had been murdered by the German S. S. troops. He enclosed a statement they had received from a soldier in the same group who had escaped. It read.

On June 8th 1945, when a prisoner of war,
I along with a number of gunners and infantry men were herded together in a field.
The enemy then appeared with machine carbines and began to fire at us.
Several of us made a dash to escape and I was fortunate enough to get away.
Those in front were hit by the first burst and this
gave us in the rear a chance to run.
I don't think any of the front had a chance for there were eleven enemy firing machine carbines.
Two members of the Royal Winnipeg Rifles
escaped with me and they could probably identify
the names of the others missing from their unit.

The letter went on. In order to erase any doubt in your mind that your husband is dead, It can now be stated that the thirty one bodies were positively identified. It is requested please, that this information be not made public as the investigation is in the hands of the War Crimes Investigation Committee. The letter was signed. Colonel C. L Laurin. "In charge of war recorders".

It was better for Nona to know. She had a memorial service for him in the church in Dunrea. Mother accompanied Evelyn on the piano while she sang "Someday we'll Understand" A tea was held at Grandmas after. It seemed to be some kind of closure.

Japan had surrendered and we were all confident that Germany would be next.

France was taken back by the allied forces and we were all singing songs like.

"How you gonna keep em down on the farm.
After they've seen Paree" and
"There'll be a hot time in the town of Berlin.
When our boy's go marching in"

Weeks went by and finally the word came. Germany had surrendered. Oh what excitement. After years of war it was finally over. All the towns around made huge bonfires with a dummy on top that was supposed to represent Hitler. And everyone stood around and cheered as he burned to the ground. There was dancing and singing in the streets and a wonderful feeling of relief.

Soon the troops were coming home and we were meeting the trains that carried the boys from our district. There were big concerts and home coming parties for every bunch as they arrived. We were helping with the music for these concerts and I remember an old fellow coming up to Mother at one hall and saying "Teddy you have four kids and they all look exactly the same". We didn't look that much alike. I guess it was because we were all blond with blue eyes. Mother was always called Teddy. I don't know why but even to this day my cousins refer to her as Aunt Teddy. Harvey came into Winnipeg so Uncle Ivan, Aunt Ethel and Joan and Russell went in there to meet him. His girlfriend Helen was there too and Joan told us after they were forever kissing. Who could blame them.

Nona was a brick she went to homecoming parties and did the best she could to look happy. We all wished Angus was among the boys coming home. So many happy faces and a lot of sad ones to. One French family from Dunrea had lost three sons. We were sorry to hear that Ronnie Armstrong's plane went down over the English Channel the day after the war ended. What a sad thing to happen just when the war was over. This was a time in our lives we could never forget.

CHAPTER TWENTY SIX

The war was over. It seemed impossible for us to believe. For most of our growing up years we had been at war. It had always been a fact in our lives, even if thankfully we were not in a country where the bombs were falling. It left us feeling there was nothing to do. Oh we were only to happy to throw away our ration books and not worry about how much sugar we used. And we were all very happy that all our men were back home and our adults were happy to be getting back to normal. But to us the war was normal and we had to get used to not having it to think about. We thanked God there was no more killing over there. I guess we just had to get used to a different way of life.

It didn't take us long though. Daddy was in charge of post war housing in Brandon. He also still had an office at Shilo and one at Rivers so he was very busy. Mother wanted to teach one more year but she wanted to be closer to Brandon so she left Bellafield and got the south Brandon school. This was a smaller school and she only had fifteen students. When we got there Mother rented a large house that belonged to a family named Mumby's. They lived across the road from us and we liked them very much. They had one son named Austin who was about our age.

Evelyn and Nona were both taking secretarial courses in Brandon, so they boarded in town. Buddy and I were taking grade eleven at home with Mothers help. Evelyn always came home for weekends.

Just down the road from us lived a young couple that we became good friends with. Rose and Hilton Attridge had one little girl, Joy who attended Mothers school. Rose and Hilton were a lot of fun and we spent a lot of time at their place.

Shortly after the school term began Mother planned a box social and dance to get to know the folks in the district. All the women were to make a lunch box for two and decorate it nicely. Then at the party the box's would be auctioned off to the men. Whoever bought your box you were obliged to have lunch with.

Evelyn was in town all week and would just get home in time for the party so she asked Rose and I to make her a box and decorate it. We were only to happy to. We spent a lot of time on her box. We made sandwiches for her and baked a lovely apple pie. Then we found an old hair pin with a long hair in it of course. These items we washed very carefully and stuck them in the centre of the pie. Now Evelyn had been reading a very sexy book called "Kitty", "sexy for those days anyway". We found this book and cut off the cover page and glued it onto the inside cover of her box. We then decorated the outside of her box and tied a red ribbon around it.

There was a young fellow in the district that Evelyn liked and we were quite sure he felt the same, so our next move was to let him know exactly what her box looked like so he could bid on it and our work was done. Then we did our boxes. Hilton knew which one was Roses. And I'm sure he told Austin which one was mine as that was who I got for lunch. Anyway Evelyn was really mad at us for awhile and she looked so embarrassed that we didn't let it go on too long before we went over and told them what we had done. We also told them they could eat the pie as we had really cleaned the hair pin and it was only on one side anyway. She was still a little angry but Howard thought it was funny. The money that was raised went to buy new books for the school. Mother said the school library was a joke.

We had a phone for the very first time. It was a party line with five other parties but we thought it was great. We found out very soon that we could listen in to other conversations and while we were not interested in most of them, we did like to know were the house parties were and who was going so in the event that we were invited we could decided if it was going to be a good one. Another thing we liked about having a phone was we could contact Evelyn in town if we were trying to learn a new song and try it out for her. We would get around the phone with our old instruments and play and sing it to her and she would tell us if we were doing it right. I suppose this was how Austin found out that we played and sang together, which only proved that we were not the only ones listening in on the phone. Anyway, as a result he was over nearly every night, especially on weekends when Evelyn was home. We found that he and his father were very fond of music and loved just coming over, even if we were just practising something.

Mother had found a Swiss song in a music book that we were trying to learn. It was not easy as the chorus was a Swiss yodel and while we had tried a few country yodels this was different. Then mother told us we had to try the yodel in harmony and that was hard. We usually ended up laughing half way through. Austin and his Dad loved it.

One night Austin's father told us that there was going to be a radio contest in Sourus in about a month and we should enter. The concert was to be done first to an audience in the hall, who would then pledge so much money to there favourite performance. The top ten would then go on the radio and people at home could phone in their pledges. We were not too interested as we knew no one in Sourus and felt that the audience would be voting for people they knew. So we forgot about it.

About a month later the four of us were home alone as Mother had gone in to Brandon and was coming out later with Daddy. Now it was winter and very cold and we were just fooling around at home when a knock came at our door and there was Austin and his Father. He looked at us and said "why aren't you guys ready. You know I entered you in the radio contest at Sourus". He then insisted that we get ready and he was going to take us there. We had nothing prepared but got ourselves together and off we went. We had been working on that Swiss song so decided on the way that was what we would do. We only thought we would have to do one and felt we must make the attempt for Mr Mumby.

When our turn came up we did our number and were encored. Now we were stuck. So to keep with the same theme we went out and did an old Swiss song we had leaned years before called "From Lucerne To Waguss Town" which also had a Swiss yodel but an easier one. Then Buddy and Austin took off downtown to play pool as we were so sure we would not be on the radio. Well the numbers stared to come up on a big board and before long we noticed that the Pearson family were number three which meant we would be doing our numbers again. So Mr Mumby and Ronnie raced downtown to find the boys. We did our numbers and soon all the pledges began coming in. The first one that came in for us was from Uncle Geordie and Aunt Hazel with a message attached that read "why don't you guys tell us what your up to". Then we had ones from the rest of the family and nearly everyone from Bellafield. I guess on long winter nights everyone was listening to the radio. Mother and Daddy were stuck in a snow bank with their car radio on and Mother said Daddy laughed when he heard us and said "What are those bums doing in Sourus", but they sent in a pledge when they got home. The pledges went to the hospital. We had a lot of fun and met some people we really liked. There was another family of boys that called themselves "The Sourus Valley Playboys" they were very good and we often played with them after that night.

CHAPTER TWENTY SEVEN

In the early spring we had company from Alpine. The Peterson family. Mr and Mrs Peterson were very good friends of Mother and Daddy's and they were very happy to see them. They had their two sons with them, Bobby and Russell. The Petersons were my Godparents and we had seen a lot of them while living in Alpine. Russell had grown very tall and quite good looking. We could only hope he had grown over his desire to chase Evelyn and I into some dark corner. Anyway they stayed a few days and then were on their way. We thought that was that, but to our surprise they were back in a few days. It seemed they had taken a liking to the big old house and the farm land and had bought it. They planned to move in real soon and because the house was so large they wanted us to just stay there until Mothers term was over.

Mother and Daddy had been looking at a house in Brandon they wanted to buy but we could not move in until the end of July. So it started. Me trying to escape Russell's attentions and him following me around. I would go over to Rose and Hiltons and before long he would be there also. They thought he was nice and really he was, I was just not ready for so much attention. I would have been happier if we didn't live in the same house. Then I would not have minded seeing him maybe once a week. But all the time was to much.

One day we got word that Grandpa was very sick and the Doctor said he did not have much time left. Mother found a substitute teacher for the school and she and I left for Dunrea. Evelyn and Nona were still in Brandon and Daddy said he could be home with the boys every night. When we got to Dunrea, Aunt Ethel and Joan were there. Joan took me upstairs to see Grandpa after Mother had come down. I was so nervous for awhile I just stood in the doorway. But Grandpa called me in. He knew how badly I felt and began to talk to me. He first told me I was getting very pretty. I believe that he was just trying to calm me down so he could talk to me. He then told me not to be sad as he knew where he was going and it was alright with him. He went on to say we would all see each other again. Sorry Grandpa, I was sad anyway.

Mother and Aunt Ethel were spending most of there time with Grandma. It was a very sad time. Grandma would be sitting with Grandpa for awhile and worrying about him and the next moment she would be mad at him for not getting up. She was also forgetting what day it was and why we were all there. Later she was diagnosed with hardening of the arteries around the brain.

But now I'm sure the diagnoses would have been Alzhimers.

Joan and I kept making tea and looking after the kitchen. Three days later Grandpa got alot worse. Mother told us that his time was near. They asked us to go out and phone the rest of the family. Aunt May and Uncle Lloyd were in Brandon now and Harvey and Helen were on the farm. We phoned the school where Nona and Evelyn were as we knew Daddy was at work. Just before they left we had to call back to tell them that he was gone. Poor Aunt May, she so wanted to get to Dunrea in time so she could say goodbye to her Father. Grandpa had been one of the founders of Dunrea and was well liked. The house seemed to be full of people all the time coming to pay their respects.

Nona and I went with Uncle Ivan to the train to meet Aunt Addie and people were stopping us on the street to tell us how sorry they were.

Dunrea was made up of mostly French and Irish people and had two big church's. The United church and the Roman Catholic church. We were United, but Grandpa and the Catholic Priest had often sat together and talked over the years. The Catholic Church had much stricter rules in those days then they do now and they were not allowed to enter our church. We were so touched to find the Catholic Priest and some of the members of his church standing outside on the steps of the church when we came out after Grandpas funeral. I'm sure that things have changed over the years and now they could have come in.

When Uncle Ivan opened Grandpas safe, which no one ever went into but him while he lived, he found a stack of old unpaid accounts from the butcher shop. It seemed during the dirty thirties he had let most everyone charge their meat and never sent them a bill. He also found an envelope with five thousand dollars in it addressed to Grandma. Uncle Ivan said it should have been in the bank as that was a lot of money in those days, but Grandpa wasn't to much into banks.

The next big problem was what to do with Grandma. No one wanted to leave her alone in that big house and she was bound she was going to stay there. Joan was taking Grade eleven in town so she could stay with her for awhile anyway. So that was settled for the moment and the rest of us went home.

CHAPTER TWENTY EIGHT

Mother and Daddy had bought a house in Brandon and we were getting ready to move. It was the first place we owned since Alpine, so we were all very excited about it. 406-16th street was a big house in a nice old neighbourhood. We loved it. Six bedrooms meant we could all have our own rooms. What a treat.

Evelyn and I took the third floor, there were two rooms up there and Mother and Daddy had their room on the second floor, as well as Nona, Buddy and Ronnie. There was a door leading out to a wrap around sleeping porch where we could sleep in the summer if we wanted to. Lovely old trees lined the streets and in our yard was a huge lilac bush.

The front door led into a large veranda that ran all across the front of the house and around one side. The veranda had glass windows so it could be used all year. And best of all we were all under one roof again.

Evelyn got a job in a seed store and Nona went to work for the Chamber of Commerce. Buddy was working with Daddy on the post war housing and I got a job in a small grocery store. My job did not last long. The man who owned the store lived in an apartment at the back of the store with his wife and baby. He was always sending me into the store room and then he would follow me. While there he would be trying to kiss me and a whole lot worse. One time he even tried to pull me down on some boxes. Thank goodness someone came into the store about that time.

I was very inexperienced with this kind of behaviour and didn't know how to deal with it. One day when I came home I told Mother about him. She didn't say much except not to worry about him. I thought "boy she was no help". Daddy always liked pleasant conversation at dinner so that evening we all just talked about our work. That is all but me. After dinner Daddy got his hat and went out I thought he was going for a beer as he often went for one glass in the evening. After awhile I went to bed. Just before I went to sleep he knocked on my door and came in. He had an envelope with my pay check in it and he told me I would not be going back there to work. I guess Mother had talked to him. So I was again looking for work. Then with Daddy's help I got a job on the switchboard at the hospital. That job I liked, so all was well. We were all working except Ronnie who was still in school.

Mother was substituting at a school in Brandon so she hired a lovely lady named Mrs Sutherland to look after the house. She was great. We had never had so many cookies and cakes and home made buns in our house before and we all loved Mrs Sutherland. She could certainly give us hell though if we tracked in dirt or did not leave our room tidy. Mother would just laugh and say that she was right.

Buddy had bought Daddy's old car when Daddy got a newer one. He would take us out to Suruss to see the Romanoff family every once in awhile. This was the family we had met at the radio contest. The car didn't have a horn so Buddy would stick the trumpet he had bought out the window and use it as a horn if need be.

The Romanoff's had a bunk house outside and we would go in there and play and sing all night. Then in the wee hours of the morning their Mother and Father would come out with coffee and sandwiches and we would finally go home. It was good clean fun.

Daddy was in charge of post war housing that the ex service men could buy through the Veterans Land Act. He had to inspect all the material and look after paying all the workers. When he was real busy he would get one of us to go with him on pay day to hand out the pay checks. This made us feel very important.

One month however it got very scary as Daddy had refused to pass a whole line of houses and until he did they could not be sold and the contractors could not get paid. Daddy said there were cracks in the cement and it just wouldn't hold up. At first it wasn't too bad as I guess they were trying to bribe Daddy. One morning we woke up to a lot of noise outside and there was a crew in paving our drive way. Daddy was having breakfast and he just said, "They can pave anything they like, those houses won't be passed until they fix that cement". Then the phone calls started and they were scary. They amounted to threats. But he would not back down. He told them that his own job could be at stake if there was trouble over the cement in those homes. Finally they must have fixed everything to his liking as there were no more calls. Mother was really relived as she said she was getting a little worried.

George Romanoff got a job in Brandon and asked Mother if he could board at our place. She agreed so we put another bed in Buddy's room.

Winter was upon us and Jack's toboggan slide opened on a hill just outside of town. Two slides had been built on this hill, one was for beginners and children and the other was for adults only. At the top of the hill was a shed with a stove in it so we could come in and get warm. There they sold coffee and pop and donuts. We would go up there on Saturday nights and have a lot of fun. About six of us would get on one long toboggan and believe me the one on the end had a rough ride. George got the back one night and when I went in to have a coffee and warm up he yelled across the room "Eileen I wrecked my rectum". I was embarrassed but everyone in there seemed to think it was funny.

So from then on when anyone came up the hill they would yell "Eileen I wrecked my rectum". Finally I just laughed with them secretly wishing I could commit murder.

Aunt May and Uncle Lloyd often spent Saturday night at our place and when we got home Mother and Aunt May would have hot chocolate and hamburger's all ready for us.

Buddy had his guitar and trumpet going most of the time at home. He got himself speakers and an amplifier and he had piles of music books all over his room. He would be up most of the night studying music. He got together a little band with Evelyn on the piano and they called themselves "The Blue notes". Before long they were asked to play for the dances at the Orange Hall three nights a week. Evelyn was going with a fellow named Johnnie by this time. I really did not like him but Evelyn was in love.

CHAPTER TWENTY NINE

Ronnie quit school and went to work with Daddy. Mother was not to happy about this but Ronnie was skipping a lot of school and going to the pool hall. I guess Mother thought he would be better working. Buddy's best friend Jud was at our place a lot. He could twist Mother around his little finger, so if they ever got into trouble she never blamed Jud. One night he took Buddy and I out to one of his friends house where they were drinking beer and wine. We had never drank any of that stuff before so I guess the only way of putting it is to tell the truth. We got plastered. Jud had to almost carry us into the house where he parked us on the couch. Mothers remark when she saw us was "well I can plainly see I have you to thank for dragging them home".

We were to sick to tell her she also had him to thank for getting us drunk. Anyway he sat down with Mother and had a cup of tea. I don't know how he did that as he had had just as much to drink as we had. Oh how sick we were the next day.

Buddy was getting quite wild with a bunch of old friends of Jud's that partied a lot. They had a secret message they used when ever one of them could have a party. This was mostly when their parents were away and they had the house to themselves. The phone would ring and who ever answered would hear, "boxes and boxes of beer, barrels and barrels of wine". Then Buddy had to find out where the party was. Mother was getting very worried about Buddy. To have a party with drinks and girls it had to be a house party because in those days women were not allowed in the beer parlours or any drinking establishment in Manitoba.

Grandma was becoming unable to live alone, so Uncle Ivan sold her house for her and built a small cottage right next to their place so they could watch over her. I was visiting Joan for a few days and I realized how hard it was for Aunt Ethel even with Joan's help, as Grandma was getting very bossy and hard to get along with. We knew it was her sickness but Aunt Ethel always had so much to do. She always helped with the farm work and garden as well as look after her own house and Grandma.

One evening Joan and I were sitting with Grandma. She was lying on the bed trying to read. She had her book in one hand and the coal oil lamp in the other. The lamp would start to tip and we were scared she would drop it on the bed. We tried to get her to put the lamp on the bedside stand but she said she couldn't see well enough when it was there. The hydro wasn't out in the country yet. We told Uncle Ivan that she could burn herself up if the lamp fell and he said he to was worried about it but he didn't know what to do. He said Grandma should be in a home for seniors but the closest one was in Winnipeg. The cottage wasn't working that's for sure.

So finally Aunt May said she would take her to their place. They had bought a small house and fixed a room upstairs for Lloyd Jr., so Grandma moved into his room. We all thought this would be the answer. It lasted three months. Grandma was up roaming around most of the night and Uncle Lloyd couldn't get any sleep. He had to get up so early in the morning to go to work that he simply couldn't handle it. So she was moved to our place.

Poor Grandma she had been such a fine lady. It was so hard for everyone to see her like that. She would go out when no one noticed and get lost and everyone would be out looking for her. One time the police had to be called.

She had also become incontinent and Mother and Mrs Sutherland would have to wash her and clean her up. And this they were willing to handle, but she began to believe that people were breaking into the house and into her room. One night Evelyn had been out with Johnnie and when she was coming home Grandma came rushing down the stairs with a pair of scissors and was attacking her. Evelyn had to yell over and over "Grandma it's me, Evelyn". By this time the whole house was awake and Grandma felt so bad she was crying and Evelyn was crying and Mother was crying. The next day Mother and Aunt May went to the Doctor for some advice. He told them there was nothing they could do for her and it was only going to get worse. He said she should be in a nursing home where they could keep her safe. The only one they could get was in Winnipeg. It seemed so far away but the family got together and decided it was the only thing they could do. We all cried a little when Mother and Uncle Ivan took her away, but we knew it was the only thing to do. Loving her was not enough any more. She needed more care then we could give her.

The spring of 1947 Winnipeg had a very bad flood. Both the Red and the Assinaboine rivers overflowed their banks and hundreds of people had to leave their homes. The city of Brandon was taking in a lot of these people. They put up cots in the church's and some schools. The people of Brandon were asked to take as many of these people as possible, so we all bunked together on the second floor and the sleeping porch and Mother got the third floor ready for a family from Winnipeg. The lady, I can't remember her name now, had two little boys. Her husband brought them out and then went back to help bag up the rivers. The poor woman would come down and have tea with Mother. She was so worried about how much they were losing that she just needed someone to talk to. They were at our place for a week when her husband came back to get them. He said there wasn't as much damage to their home as they had expected, so that made his wife feel better.

Then Mother and Aunt May took the bus in to Winnipeg to see if Grandma was alright. When they arrived they found that the home had been evacuated and all the patients had been flown to Regina and were not back yet. So they stayed in Winnipeg for a couple of days until they got back. They were not very happy with the home, as they thought that at least they should have phoned and given the family the opportunity to go in and get her for the duration of the flood, as the plane trip and the strange place were very confusing for Grandma.

Joan was getting married to Angus MacDonald. It was to be quite a wedding in the church in Dunrea. Evelyn and I were to sing "Oh Promise Me" and Mother would accompany us on the piano. Mother, Daddy, Nona and Ronnie went down to Dunrea in Daddy's car. But Evelyn and I both had to work that morning, so Buddy was to bring us as soon as we got off. Now this would have worked fine except that Buddy's old car broke down half way there and we had to sit on the road until someone gave us a ride. Everyone was coming out of the church when we arrived, the Wedding was over. We felt terrible but there was nothing we could do. Anyway, they asked us to sing at the reception held at Helen and Harvey's. No music accompanied us as there was no piano there, but we bravely got up and did it. Anything for Joan.

Buddy began going with a girl named Marg. Mother was real pleased as it calmed him down alot. So Buddy, Marg, Jud and I spent alot of our time together. Evelyn and a young fellow named Mel, had a half hour radio program every Wednesday night. They were called "The Singing Sweethearts". Their theme song was "Have I Told You Lately That I Love You". Johnny was not very happy as a lot of people in town began to think they really were sweethearts.

Aunt Lydia and Uncle Adolf bought a house in Winnipeg and as soon as they moved in Aunt Lydia came to see us. We were so surprised to find she had taken up smoking. She never seemed to smoke a whole cigarette and was forever dashing around the house looking for a butt. I tried to tell cousin George this one time, but he wouldn't believe me. He said he knew Aunt Lydia would never smoke, but I knew differently.

CHAPTER THIRTY

Marg and I spent alot of our time riding our bikes when we were not working. We would ride for miles out in the country. It was nice to get out where we could see for miles. We loved the prairies. We would take our lunch and sit by a creek and talk and eat lunch. We both had always lived in the country before moving to town. Marg's family had been on a farm. Her older sister was mentally challenged and her parents thought she would be better in town. I always knew there were things Marg wasn't telling me about that, but after all it was her business. I found out a few months later, that her sister had been raped by a farm hand who lived close to them and maybe that was what made them want to move into town. In any event they were a very nice family and very devoted Roman Catholics.

On most of our rides out in the country we had to pass a huge brick building. This building looked so cold and foreboding. We found out later that it was a boarding school for Indian children. The children from the reserves were brought in there to live and go to school. The children there were lonely and not treated as well as they should have been. I believe foreboding was a good word for that place. Do buildings like that give off some kind of unpleasant vibes? I don't know, but we felt something passing that place. Anyway, it is long gone now and that's a good thing.

One day we rode around one of the buildings that Buddy was working on. They were all up on the roof working, so we started to tease Buddy about falling off as it was so windy. At three o'clock we headed for home as I had told Mother I would help her with supper. Mrs. Sutherland was away and Mother wanted to work in the garden. Mother and I had just got things started and were taking a cold drink out to the veranda when we saw a taxi drive into the yard. The driver got out and was trying to help Buddy out of the car. Mother took one look at Buddy and told the driver to leave him in the car. We got in and headed for the hospital. Buddy had fallen off the roof and landed on the hard cement. He was badly hurt.

Nona, Evelyn and Ronnie were home when Daddy got home. He had gone to check on the job and the men had told him what had happened. He had thought that Buddy had been taken right to the hospital and was just coming to get Mother. So they all arrived at the hospital while the Doctors were still working on Buddy. Daddy was really angry at the men for not sending him right to the hospital in the first place.

He said any idiot could tell he needed medical attention.

Buddy had head injuries and broken ribs and spent several weeks in the hospital. When he was sent home he was not able to work for several months, so he spent that time working on his music and tormenting the rest of us. He loved to tease Daddy. There was a certain radio program that Daddy hated. I don't remember the guys name, but he sang country songs in a slow mournful voice. His theme song was "The Streets of Lorado", all about a dying cowboy. Before Daddy would get home after work Buddy would place his loud speakers in the hall downstairs. Then just as the program began he would run upstairs and turn on the radio full blast. Daddy would yell "turn that off you bum" and Buddy would laugh. Daddy would laugh too, mostly I believe because he was so glad to see Buddy back to his old self.

Aunt Addie came to spend a few weeks with us. She had married her boss, quite late in life and they had a little boy named Donald. Uncle Harry had managed General Motors in Calgary for years and had finally been sent back to Oshawa Ontario where the head office was. Donald was four when he came with his Mother to visit. He was a cute little fellow and we all loved him, but he was a very active little guy. He loved to get up to Buddy's room and turn on the radio and Buddy's speakers. Someone always had to dash up and get him before he got into Buddy's music and had it all over.

Aunt Addie was a beautiful piano player. Before she left Calgary she had a radio program every night. It was called "Memories with Addie". In the evenings we loved to get her to play for awhile. I loved to hear her play "Kitten on the Key" and "Nola", she just seemed to be all over the piano. We hated to see them leave when the time came. They lived so far away we did not get to see them much.

CHAPTER THIRTY ONE

About ten miles out of Brandon there was a steep hill going down to a pretty little valley. A lovely little river ran along the valley at the bottom of the hill. Along it's bank was an open air dance hall. The hall opened as soon as it was warm enough in the spring and closed for the winter. We liked to go out to the dances there on the weekend as they always had a good band. One night in mid June Buddy, Marg, Jud and I were on our way out there when a freak snow storm came up suddenly. This was certainly not likely to happen at that time of the year, but soon the roads became very slippery. Cars were sliding into the ditch all over and before long we were also in the ditch. Try as we might we could not get back on the road, so we were forced to stay there until morning when we could catch a bus back into town. The bus was packed as it kept picking up people along the road who were in the same predicament. I was a little concerned about explaining being out all night to Mother and Daddy, as any time we were going to be really late we would phone. When I got home Daddy was just putting out the milk bottles. All he said was "good morning Eileen". I said "you know I can explain this", but he just said I better get some sleep and we would talk later. He always

161

had complete trust in us. By the time I got up Buddy had already told them all about it and of course there was still a little snow on the ground.

A tattoo artist set up shop in town and Buddy, Ronnie and Jud wanted to go and see him. Mother told Buddy and Ronnie she did not want to see any tatoos on them when they got back. The next night we were all going to a big house party. Even Nona was going this time which was a bit unusual. Jud always called me Annie ever since we had gone to the movie "Annie Get Your Gun", so when we got to the party he began showing off his tattoo. It was a circle of flowers with Annie printed in the centre. Well I did not want my name on his arm for life, even if it wasn't my real name, everyone knew what he called me. I was really angry and told him I would have nothing to do with him until he removed it. Now it is not easy to get a freshly done tattoo taken off, so the next day he was over and showed me what he had done. He had gone and had the Annie covered with flowers and under it he had a R.I.P. for rest in peace. Then he told everyone that he had buried Annie. I decided that I could live with that.

The theatre on main street had midnight movies that we sometimes went to. One night there seemed to be a lot of white balloons flying around and Marg and I were batting at them until

Evelyn told us to leave them alone. She said they were condoms, we were totally disgusted.

Then again another night when we had decided to go to the movies, as the movie was one we were wanting to see, Buddy and Jud were downstairs making themselves a sandwich when they came across some garlic cloves that Mother had got to put in some pickles she was going to make. So they decided to play a real trick on everyone and they ate a couple of garlic sandwiches. When we smelled them we would not even go into the theatre with them. So when we walked in, Evelyn, Johnnie, Marg, Ronnie and I, we made sure we sat where there were no seats for them left. When they came along they found a few seats where alot of other people were sitting. After awhile we looked back and found that everyone near them had moved and there they sat by themselves. They thought it was extremely funny.

Evelyn and Johnnie had set their wedding date for November eighth. We all thought she was making a mistake but she would hear none of that. Nona was to be her matron of honour and I would be her brides maid. I was also to sing while they were signing the register. The song she picked was very difficult. It was "Thine Alone" from the operetta Eileen. Mother went out and bought the sheet music, as she would

163

accompany me on the piano. It was going to take a lot of practise.

CHAPTER THIRTY TWO

Our house had a coal and wood furnace in the basement. The vents went to every room. It was nice in the winter to come in out of the cold and stand in front of a vent and let the warm air blow up on your legs. When we moved in we had an ice box in the kitchen. Once a week the iceman came to change the ice. He would come down the street ringing his bell. He had an ice wagon pulled by an old horse. This horse would stand still while his master carried the big blocks of ice into the houses and deposit them into the top of the ice box. The ice man didn't seem to even have to drive the horse, he would just jump on the wagon when he finished at one house and the horse would plod on to the next. We also had a coal and wood stove in the kitchen. There was a coal chute in the basement. When the coal was getting low Mother would call the coal man and he would bring a truck load and dump it down the chute. But we had indoor plumbing and electricity and that was a far cry from Alpine or Bellafield.

One day after we had been in the house about a year, mother sent the boys out to chop some wood for the kitchen stove. They went out and got to it, grumbling all the way. While they were at it Mother went downtown to do some shopping. When she came back she had bought a new electric stove and refrigerator. We were all so thrilled with them, but the boys thought she could have let them know before they cut all that wood.

Jud spent most of his time at our place and he and the boys seemed to be doing something in the basement most of the time when they weren't working. We were all pretty tired of the noise and banging they were doing and were glad when it stopped. Daddy finally said he had better go down and see what they were up to. When he came up he was laughing and said they had made a room down there. We had all been wondering, but they had asked us not to snoop. Anyway, we were all glad they were done so we could get some sleep at night. Well we must have been dreaming as the next night we woke up to an awful smell of paint coming up to our rooms through the vents. Nona, Evelyn and I had really had enough. We got on our housecoats and were on our way down there to kill them. But Daddy intervened and told us the house was warm enough so we should turn off our vents and leave the boys alone. So we did and opened our windows and went back to sleep. The next day we were invited down to see their handy work. Somewhere there must have been a sale on blue paint, because everything was blue. The ceiling was blue, the walls were blue, the night table was blue, the clock was blue, the radio was blue, the picture frames were blue and the bedsteads were blue. Daddy came upstairs laughing and said "those bums are crazy" and went to work. We named it the blue room of course and it remained the blue room for as long as we lived at home.

Buddy and Marg had stopped going together but remained very good friends. Buddy had a big crush on a girl that worked with me at the hospital. This girl had a boyfriend and paid very little attention to Buddy's advances, but he never stopped trying. So one day while Marg and I were downtown we happened to see Buddy's car parked on the street. This gave us the idea to play a trick on him. We bought some nice pink paper, an envelope and a small bottle of perfume. Then Marg wrote a note as Buddy would know my handwriting. She put in the note that she was so depressed because she had broken up with her boyfriend and could he meet her at the coffee shop at the bus depot at eight o'clock and signed the note with this girl's name. Then we went for supper. Marg made sure she could have supper at our place to see what happened.

We could hardly help but laugh when we saw him getting ready. He showered and shaved and spent the longest time in front of the mirror combing his hair. Of course we kept asking him where he was going, but he wouldn't say. After he left we waited for about half an hour and walked down to the coffee shop. There he sat at the counter waiting. As soon as he saw us he gave us a dirty look and got up and left. I guess he caught on. Mother said it was a dirty trick, but we knew he would get even.

One day at work I found a book in one of the waiting rooms at the hospital. Since it was Sunday and very slow at work, I took it into our office to read. The title of the book was "The Strange Loves of Vickie Saunders". I had read a few chapters when my relief girl came. She saw what I was reading and said she had read a little of it too, so we spent awhile together trying to figure out what it was all about. We read a little together and finally she said "what on earth are these women doing" and we started to laugh. Just then one of the younger Doctors came in to book an operation and saw what we were reading. He asked us what was so funny and we told him that we couldn't figure out what this book was all about. He was so great with us, he sat down and told us that but for the grace of God anyone of us could have been born in the wrong sex and how hard it was for those people. He told us that down in the States they had big clubs and things for them and that one day he hoped there would be places like that for them in Canada. He explained it so well that we could never make jokes or laugh about them again, as we realized that they were people just like us only a little different. I have always been thankful to him for explaining this so well to a couple of very ignorant girls. In those days there was so much that never was talked about and we had never come across that subject before.

Our elevator boy at the hospital became a very good friend to all of us. His name was Teddy and he was a really nice kid, just out of school. He loved music and singing and would go out to the old gravel pit with a bunch of us and play and sing for hours. He would try to learn the guitar with Buddy's help and claimed he would one day get good enough to play in his band.

No one knew when Teddy started to get sick. I believe he tried to cover it up. The staff dining room was one floor down from our office and we would always get Teddy to take us down at lunch time. One day I got on the elevator with him and I could see he was sick. I have never to this day seen such large drops of sweat. They were the size of a dime. I tried to get him to tell me what was wrong but he said he would be all right in a minute. When I came to work the next day Teddy was being admitted. I asked the floor nurse what was wrong with him and she told me they were running some tests, but it was likely the flu.

Our office gave out the condition reports when families would call in to see how someone was, so we always got a sheet of reports every morning. When I came to work the morning after

Teddy was admitted there was a red star by his name. I assumed it was a mistake and got hold of Mrs. Hannah the head nurse. She had tears in her eyes when she told me there was no mistake and to make sure all the girls knew not to give out a report on his condition. Only the Doctor was to give that report. She said that Teddy was dying. When they had done the chest x-ray they had found his lungs were like a snow field. I couldn't believe it. Somehow I got through the day, but when I got home I just sobbed in Mothers arms. She told me it was always hardest the first time someone of your own age group was dying. Buddy, Ronnie, Evelyn, Johnnie and I went to Teddy's funeral. The church was so crowded that a lot of people could not get in and had to stand outside. They put speakers out so everyone could hear the service. Somehow, I have always remembered Teddy and the total shock of his passing. He was only eighteen.

CHAPTER THIRTY THREE

Evelyn's wedding was fast approaching on November the eighth. Everyone at our place was getting ready for the big event. Nona and I went downtown to shop for our dresses. Nona got a nice dress in pale pink which was no big surprise to me, as pink was always her favourite colour. Now I on the other hand would really have liked red, but I didn't think that would go over to well, so I settled for yellow. Mother and I practicedmy song every day and it was getting easier. I found the verse a bit boring, but when it changed keys for the chorus it was quite nice. It was quite high and a little difficult to sing so I was very nervous about it. Ronnie kept telling me that if I got stuck I could always swing into a chorus of "Sweet Georgia Brown". It didn't help.

We were all a little worried about how this marriage was going to turn out, but since it was going to happen anyway we were all trying to do the best we could. The day of the wedding Nona was helping Evelyn get dressed and she told Mother afterwards that Evelyn did not look as happy as she thought a bride should. She said she told Evelyn that if she had any doubts to let her know and she would put her on a bus to Winnipeg and she could spend awhile with Angus's family. She even said she would go to the church and call off the wedding, but Evelyn insisted on going through with it. I guess she felt she had to, as unknown to us she was pregnant. At that time that was such a big disgrace. If she had only trusted us as a family, we would have understood and it would have saved her alot of heartache. The last thing Daddy said to her as we were going into the church was "remember you always have a home". She was going to need it.

Evelyn looked lovely as she came into the church and she was smiling. I guess all her doubts had vanished when she saw Johnnie. Her dress was white satin and rather form fitting. Her hair was very blond and curly. She wore a small vial with a band of apple blossoms, artificial of course as it was November. Her flowers were red roses and she made a beautiful bride. Buddy and Ronnie were ushers and Johnnie's brother Hugh stood up for him as best man. Hugh was a very nice guy and worked hard. Johnnie's father was also very nice. He had worked for the railway for years. Johnnie had two sisters who also seemed nice. This left his mother, who was loud and bossy and managed the family with an iron will. Johnnie seemed to be her favourite and in her eyes could do no wrong. Mrs. Sutherland was very busy getting the reception lunch ready and as usual it was lovely.

Now, to speak of drinks. There was a lovely fruit punch downstairs and the only hard drinks in the house were one bottle of whiskey that Daddy had upstairs. He would take the men up one at a time and give them a drink. That was the only liquor I had ever seen in our home. All our Aunts and Uncles and cousins were there. Aunt Lydia had even come out from Winnipeg. We also had a few close friends like Marg and Jud. The house was packed. Evelyn changed into a nice wine suit for going away and off they went to Winnipeg for a few days.

CHAPTER THIRTY FOUR

Mother was the most honest lady I have ever met. She would not lie to anyone and was very upset if anyone lied to her. One cold winter night her honesty was put to the test. She and Daddy had just come home from the market with alot of groceries and had begun to put them away. Mother had put in a long day at school and just wanted to get finished, have a bath and go to bed. But she couldn't find a package of meat she had bought. In this package was a roast, some cold meat and wieners. She searched for awhile and then took the bill back to the market and told them she did not get her meat. They were very obliging and got the meat that was on her bill and gave it to her. When she got home Nona had found the first package. It had gotten under the table and some paper had fallen on top of it. Well, she hummed and hawed for awhile as she really didn't feel like another trip to the market. But finally she said I will never sleep if I don't go back with this meat, so poor Daddy had to get up and take her back to give the second package of meat back to the store. That was Mother's way.

Evelyn and Johnnie had moved into an apartment not to far from our place. Evelyn was sick alot through her pregnancy. Johnnie was driving a truck for "Coke a Cola" at this time and was out of town alot. He didn't make much money and blew most of what he did make. Marriage had not affected his social life in the slightest. Evelyn was still playing for the dances with Buddy. This was the only money she got to buy the things she needed for the baby. She would buy material and Mother would help her make diapers and things. When Johnnie was home he lay on the bed and read comic books. Very soon after the wedding he found an old apartment building that they could look after and get their rent free. It was hard work and Evelyn had to do most of it as Johnnie was seldom home. There was a huge furnace in the basement that she had to go and shovel coal into several times a day.

Little Billy was born on June the fourth. He couldn't even be late. Johnnie's mother told Mother that it certainly wasn't Johnnie's fault the baby was conceived before they were married. That it was up to the girl to look after that. She was a real winner, that one.

Billy was a beautiful baby. He was all pink and white and about eight pounds, so she could not say he was premature. By this time none of us cared, he was so adorable. About that time a lady from child welfare arrived at Evelyn's door and told her that a very young girl out in the country was pregnant and had named Johnnie as the father. Johnnie claimed innocence of course and I don't know how that turned out, as his mother went to bat for him. There was very little they could do to prove a thing like that in those days. Evelyn was very unhappy, but she thought she had made her bed so she must stay. We had never had a divorce in our family and I guess she did not want to be the first.

Then one night I was down at her place and saw how sickly she looked. After alot of questions she finally told me she was pregnant again. She said Johnnie had forced himself on her when Billy was only a few weeks old. She had not seen a Doctor as she said Johnnie had got Daddy to co-sign a loan to pay for Billy's birth and she had found out he spent the money and never paid the Doctor or the hospital. She didn't feel she could go and see the Doctor until his last bill was paid. Then she made me promise not to tell Mother and Daddy. However, things came to a head one night when Mother and Daddy along with Aunt May and Uncle Lloyd dropped in to see her. Johnnie and his friends were in the kitchen playing cards and drinking beer and since there was only a large kitchen and a bedroom they found Evelyn in the bedroom with the baby. Mother and Daddy were angry, but did not want to say anything. Then one night at supper we were all talking about how badly Evelyn was being treated. Daddy didn't say much, but just as we were finishing up he turned to the boys and I and quietly said "go and get your sister, I want to talk to her". We did, and as a result Evelyn and Billy never went back to that apartment or to Johnnie.

Very soon after Evelyn left him we began to hear nasty stories that were floating around town about Evelyn and we knew they were started by Johnnie. We tried to ignore them, but they only got worse and soon were involving other men. I guess that's when Buddy had had enough. So one day when he came home with a black eye we knew he had been to see Johnnie. Mother thought Buddy should not have got into a fight, but Daddy said he wished he had been the one to do it. As it turned out I guess Johnnie had got the worst of it and his Mother was ready to sue. But that soon died down and we heard no more about it. Then Daddy went down and paid the Doctor and the hospital for Billy's birth and paid in advance for the new baby. The only thing he asked of Evelyn was never to have Johnnie around our place again. I don't think that was going to be much of a problem.

Gerald Wayne was born on April thirteenth, just ten months after Billy's birth. Evelyn had a very difficult time having Gerry, as it was a breach birth and Evelyn was not in good condition. The two boys were so much alike in looks that people were always mistaking them for twins. But their personalities were as different as night and day. Where Billy was sweet and quiet and easy to look after, Gerry was demanding and mischievous. He would throw his food around and laugh at us trying to pick it up. He was funny and cute and just a little nasty but we loved all his silly ways. Daddy got Evelyn to take Johnnie to court for some support for the boys. She did and the Judge very generously told Johnnie he had to give her fifty dollars a month for the two of them. Big deal. Even fifty dollars would have helped her though. But Johnnie left town rather than pay.

That same year Ronnie had a bad experience. He was coming home from a friends house late one night when he saw Jud on the street, so he picked him up and was going to take him to his home. Jud had been drinking and on the way home he asked Ronnie to pull over for a minute. Ronnie thought he was just going to relieve himself so he sat in the car and waited. They were beside some warehouses and Ronnie said he noticed that Jud was carrying something when he got back in the car, but he was in a hurry to get home so he just drove on.

The next morning the police were at our door. Someone had seen Ronnie's car and I guess they saw Jud in it. It seems Jud had broken into a meat packing place and stolen some steaks. I think the story went that he was going to make a snack when he got home and the meat packing place happened to be right there. The police arrested both Jud and Ronnie. Jud tried to tell the Judge that Ronnie had nothing to do with it, but he didn't believe him. They were sent to prison for three months. We were all devastated as we knew that Ronnie was innocent, but there was nothing anyone could do. Daddy would go up and see him every Sunday. Mother would never go. She could not see one of her children in jail. She would however, fix a big box of goodies and Ronnie would share them with Jud.

We were all really upset with Jud, but Ronnie didn't seem to be holding a grudge so we tried to get over it. Buddy was furious with him though and it took awhile for him. He would go and see Ronnie but would have nothing to do with Jud. Maybe for Jud it was a good thing, as he had been drinking too much and somehow we all knew he would not have done such a thing sober. Anyway, the three months passed and they were home again. Buddy did forgive Jud after he had told him how stupid he was a few times and they got back to life as usual.

CHAPTER THIRTY FIVE

Evelyn was not well after Gerry was born and had to go back to the hospital. This left Mother and Nona and I to look after the two babies. Mother looked after Gerry as he was still so little and Nona and I took charge of Billy. He was so sweet and good, we loved to dress him up and take him downtown with us.

I had changed jobs by then and was working at the paper. My boss was called Shad by everyone and all the staff were very fond of him. I worked in the printing section right next to the sports editors office. The owner of the paper was Bob and he was quite the ladies man.

One day Marg came and asked me to go to a house party with her. She said she had met a nice man who had asked her to go and she didn't want to go alone as she did not know him that well. Well Bob was certainly surprised when he saw me. He was also embarrassed as he knew that I was aware that he was married with two children who were at the lake for a couple of weeks. I got a hold of Marg and told her and we left. I had a time getting her out of there as she really wanted to throw a few things at him, but somehow I managed. She was glad I had come along as she said she might have made a real fool of herself. She really believed everything he said.

I was a little worried about going back to work, but as soon as I got there in the morning I told Shad and he just laughed and said it served Bob right and to forget about it as Bob certainly would.

We had a baseball team come to Brandon from the States to play against some Canadian teams that summer. Alot of them were Negros and were really good players. One of the team looked after bringing the reports to the sports editor after each game. We all really liked him and always had coffee ready for when he got there, so we could visit for awhile. I really considered him a good friend.

Alot of the wilder girls in town were chasing these boys and making fools of themselves. When the team left that year they left quite a few little dark babies. It got so if you were seen talking to them at a dance or even downtown your reputation was at risk. One night Marg and I were at the dance with Jud and Buddy and Ronnie. This young member of the team was there and came over and asked me for a dance. I am sorry to say I refused. I guess I will always be ashamed of myself for that. He asked me as a friend and I was to afraid of what my friends and brothers would think. It wasn't him, I was just afraid of being classed with the girls who were always chasing after them. I will always feel bad he looked so hurt. I tried to explain it to him, but of course he didn't understand and was never my friend again. I swore I would never be such a coward again.

Mother could sew anything, but for some reason none of us girls had been interested in sewing. But one day Nona and I went to her and said we wanted to sew something if she would get the machine ready for us. She was only to happy to and told us we should start on an apron. We did not want to start on an apron, we planned to make a coat. She just laughed at us, but we were bound and determined it would be a coat. We told her we would get a pattern and then all we had to do was lay the material out on the table and cut around the pattern. We realized the lining may make it harder, but if we followed the pattern what could go wrong. Mother said go ahead but don't come to me when you get stuck. Well we cut out all the pieces and that went easy enough, but then we started to sew it together. We began to have trouble right away. Nothing looked right and after much work we found ourselves in a real mess. We asked Mother for help but she refused. Nona had a friend who could sew so we carted the whole thing over to her to see where we went wrong. after she had a good laugh she said she would do the best she could to fix it, but she didn't want our help. So we left it in her hands. When we got it back it was a coat all right, but it never really looked good. We wore it once in a while just to prove a point, but it was never a thing of beauty. And that was the end of our sewing career.

Evelyn was still playing for the dances at the orange hall with Buddy. The little money she got there and her family allowance was all she was living on with the two boys.

She had one bad habit. Like Mother she was never ready to go anywhere on time. She would sit and play canasta with Daddy until suddenly she would look at her watch and say "oh gosh, I have to be at the hall in two hours". Then she would hurry and bathe, wash her hair and set it and be fussing around trying to get her hair dry in time. There were no hair dryers in those days. She would get out the vacuum and blow air on it. Daddy would say, "why don't you start a little earlier" and she would claim she had too much to do with two babies to look after. But Daddy wasn't buying that. He would tell her in the first place the babies were in bed long ago and that Mother had put them to bed. Someone else always did when she had to play. Somehow she always made it to the hall in time.

Household Finance was always calling her about a loan Johnnie had made and never paid. They didn't know where he was, so they went after her. One time when they called she told them she would give them her family allowance. She was at Aunt Mays when they tracked her down. Aunt May was sick in bed when they came, but when Evelyn told her what it was about, she jumped out of bed and dashed out to the kitchen with her housecoat billowing behind her. She told them that Evelyn would give them her family allowance this time only, because she had said she would, but they were never to come after her for more money. They would have to find Johnnie, as that was just about all she had to live on and she had two babies. She must have put the fear of God into them as they never again asked her for money.

I was going to the Firemen's ball with the fire chief's son Jim. I had bought a new dress for this big occasion. It was midnight blue with a wide skirt that took two matching crinolines. Jim brought me a corsage of red roses and I felt very elegant until I got to the ball and started to move around a bit more. My dress made swishing noises every time I walked. I would dance "swish, swish", I would sit down "swish, swish". At one time Jim asked me "what's that noise"? I was so embarrassed. I was glad when it was over.

Nona also had a date for this ball and her date had a friend, so she talked Evelyn into going with them as a partner for this friend. Evelyn immediately took a dislike to this boy, so both her and I had a miserable time.

Anyway, Jim seemed to have the time of his life and never seemed to notice my dress problem. We went out many times after that until he went away to work and he often mentioned what a great time we had at the Firemen's ball.

In the early summer that year, Polio broke out in Brandon. It was just the year before they came out with the vaccine. The sickness really hit hard in Brandon and the surrounding towns. Everyone was scared of it. Bob, from the paper, was one of the first ones to get it and he died within a couple of days, leaving a lovely wife and two small children. It was very sad. We all had to attend his funeral. One girl we knew from the dances died right away too, leaving a husband and children. There were alot of deaths and alot of people left paralysed.

One day we found wee Billy very sick and stiff. One of us sat with him all the time. We were very scared. In a few days he started to get better and was soon his old self. Mother was sure he had a slight case of it and so was the Doctor. I believe we were just lucky.

CHAPTER THIRTY SIX

I had three weeks holidays coming in August and Marg was taking her holidays at the same time. We had been saving our money so we could take a trip to Vancouver, B.C., by bus. It was going to take us two days and a night to get there. On the day of our departure we packed a big lunch for the bus so we could save our money.

We were really looking forward to seeing the mountains. Coming from the prairies we had no idea how high they really were, so when we arrived at the foothills we thought they were the mountains. But we sure knew the difference when we got to the real thing. Everything thrilled us. The big bridges, the tunnels and most of all the beautiful mountains with their little waterfalls running down the side and the sight of wildlife we could see in the bushes if we looked hard enough. We saw our first bear and that was a big event and later, at one spot a herd of elk were grazing at the side of the road.

We stopped for a while at Frank's Slide and were awe stricken by the sight of the huge rocks that had come down on that little town. Our driver told us about a little girl who had been found beside the road after the slide and that they never knew who she had belonged to. We were getting tired by this time, but were afraid if we went to sleep we would miss something. We were fascinated with British Columbia and at every stop we would buy postcards to send home as none of our family members had seen this lovely province.

The highways have improved alot since the late 1940's. At that time they were much narrower and mostly unpaved. Going around those narrow curves with what looked to us like a mile drop over the side made us very nervous. The driver had to blow his horn when we got to a curve so the traffic on the other side would know we were coming and could pull over and stop. Of course the traffic was not nearly as heavy as it is now.

We arrived at the coast in the early morning and were disappointed that we couldn't see the ocean from the bus. We went over the Patullo bridge and were amazed at the size of it. It seemed so huge to us. The bus had to stop at a toll booth and pay to go over the bridge. This seemed very strange to us, to have to pay to go over a bridge.

As soon as we got into Vancouver we registered at a hotel. We were so tired that we really needed a good sleep, but the next day we found the Y. W. C. A., and stayed there as it was alot cheaper.

The day after we arrived we got a bus to White Rock, as the desk clerk had told us we would get a really good view of the ocean there. We found later that the ocean was all around us and we really didn't have to go that far, but it was a nice trip and we liked White Rock, so that was fine. While there we sat on a big rock and ate the most delicious meal of fish and chips. We heard the Indian legend about how the big white rock that sat on the shore was thrown over the water from Blaine Washington by an Indian brave to impress his lover.

We spent a lot of time in Stanley Park and took a trip up to Grouse mountain. Most of our meals we ate at a White Spot close to the Y. At that time White Spots were all cafeteria style and quite inexpensive. The neon sign in front was of a little man in a chef's hat chasing a cup and saucer around in a circle. The neon signs at that time were large and very active and at night the streets were all lit up with them. It looked so beautiful to us prairie chickens. It was truly amazing.

One night we were invited to a beach party at Lumberman's Arch. The bunch we went with had some beer and we were all having a good time. There was another bunch partying a little ways down the beach from us and we got to talking and kidding around with them. One of the girls in their bunch seemed really out of it and

I thought she had just had a little to much to drink. anyway, she got talking to me and asked what we were doing. I told her we were just having a few beers. She said "oh we have some stuff that is alot better than booze". I had no idea what she was talking about, so I asked her and she told me they were on drugs. I had never heard of such a thing so I told one of our group what she had said. He explained it to me and said he thought we had better pack up and go home, so we did.

What a wonderful holiday we had. We really loved B. C. Little did I know then that I would be back and spend the rest of my life in beautiful B. C. Anyway, all to soon it was time to go home, so we took the train and headed back to Manitoba.

CHAPTER THIRTY SEVEN

We were glad to be home and to tell everyone about our great trip and all the wonderful things we had seen. Then it was back to work and life went on as usual. Marg and I spent alot of time with Buddy, Ronnie and Jud, but Marg was still having a hard time getting used to the fact that Buddy was only a friend. I guess she never really got over him, even when he started to go with a cute little girl. Sometimes she would chase him until he took her out and then she would think they were back together, until she saw him out with someone else. It was quite confusing.

After a few months I saw a change in Marg. I knew she was very unhappy. She was very pale and didn't want to go anywhere or do anything. About a month later she came over one day and wanted to talk. She told me she was pregnant and who was responsible and I was in total shock. For a while I could not believe it. I confronted him right away and he was very upset. He said he would marry Marg, but she felt she could not do that as she knew he didn't love her. She also felt she could not tell her family. They were strict Roman Catholics and it would be a terrible thing for them. She told me she would rather commit suicide and I knew she meant it. I was really afraid for her. So I told her I would go away with

her. We got together all the money we could, quit
our jobs and told our folks we were going to Port
Arthur Ontario, as Marg had a job offer there and
I wanted to see the Great Lakes. It seemed like a
weak excuse, but they bought it, so that was a
start and we were on our way. I hated to lie to
Mother and Daddy, but I had to keep them from
finding out who the father of Marg's baby was, as
well as help Marg. I guess I was doing it as much
for him as for Marg and he helped us as much as
he could. At that time it was a terrible thing to
have a child out of wedlock and I must say it
always was the girl who suffered the most.

We arrived in Port Arthur with enough
money left to rent a small suite in a private home.
After we had bought a supply of grocery's we
were very close to broke. The next thing we had
to do was find some kind of work. Marg got a job
in a five and ten cent store and I got work at
Marshell Wells. Marshell Wells was a large
hardware store and I found that I liked this kind
of work very much.

Port Arthur and Fort William were twin cities
at the head of the Great Lakes in Ontario. They
have since become one city, called Thunder Bay.

After we had been there a while we had
company from Brandon. Jud arrived late one
day, so we had to tell him what was going on and
make him swear to keep our secret. He stayed for
a week and slept on our couch. We were glad to

see anyone from home. The three of us would sit on the pier at the lake in the evenings and sing "Shrimp Boats Are A Coming", a song that was popular at the time and we were trying to learn. We missed him when he left, as we felt so alone with our problem.

We spent a lonely Christmas, but we did the best we could. We got a little tree and a nice little chicken for dinner and opened the gifts that had come from home. We made sure we sent gifts and cards home and kept writing cheerful letters home so no one would guess we had a problem.

Time dragged on and Marg seemed to be sick most of the time. She soon found she could not work, but I was making a good wage so we could get by. One day our landlady came up to see us. She was very diplomatic about it, but let us know she was aware of our problem and wanted to help in anyway she could. We were very thankful. She then asked if Marg had a doctor and Marg said she was too ashamed to go to one, so she gave us the name of a nice lady doctor and talked Marg into going. She also wanted to know if Marg had any plans as to what to do after the baby was born. Marg really didn't know what to do. She wanted to keep the baby but didn't know how that would be possible. Our landlady then went downstairs and phoned a lady at Children's Services, just to come and talk to Marg. A few days later while I was at work a woman came to see Marg. Marg told me she was really nice and stayed most of the afternoon. She had advised Marg to give the baby up for adoption. She assured her that she would get the baby a good home and when Marg told her she had not gone to a doctor as she had no health insurance. She made an appointment and took her to see a doctor right away.

A few days later she came again to tell Marg she had a family who wanted to adopt a baby, all lined up. She said they were a lovely couple who could not have children and the baby would have a good home. She said they were willing to pay all Marg's medical bills. So Marg agreed it would be the best thing to do. Without these wonderful people, I don't know what we would have done as we seemed to be just drifting along before then.

So one day in the early spring I came home from work and the landlady told me we must take Marg to the hospital. The lady from family services came and took us to the hospital. She told us that she had contacted the adoptive parents and they were on their way to the hospital. Marg felt bad that she could not even meet them or see the baby after it was born, but at that time those were the rules. I stayed in the hospital until the baby was born and then sat with Marg till early morning. She was so upset. I tried to assure her she had done the right thing for him. Our landlady came to get me about seven and we hung around until Marg had gone to sleep. When I got home I called work and booked off for the day and went to bed. I cried myself to sleep that day. I cried for a baby I would never know; who was my nephew. I believe that was the day I grew up.

CHAPTER THIRTY EIGHT

We stayed in Port Arthur for about a month after Marg's baby was born so Marg could get stronger and put the whole thing behind her a bit. I really liked my job and hated to give notice, but I also wanted to get home. One big problem was money, as we had been living on my wage alone for some time and by the time we paid everything up we had very little left. So we packed all our clothes and sent them home on the bus and decided to hitchhike home from Ontario. At that time hitchhiking was a lot safer than it is now and young people went all over the country that way. We had never tried it before so we were a little nervous but we didn't want to phone home for money as they would certainly wonder why we were so broke, as they thought we had both been working. So one nice sunny morning we took off. People stopped to pick up hitchhikers in those days and we made sure we only got into cars with a family or at least an older couple. Mother had written me that Daddy would be in Winnipeg at a big conference that week, so we made sure we would be there while he was still in town. It was a long trip, but we met some very nice people on the way.

When we arrived in Winnipeg we were tired and I'm sure in need of a bath, but we went right to the Regent Hotel where we knew Daddy would be. It seemed they were talking about a big project in Churchill when we arrived, and the conference room was filled with tables and well dressed men. Daddy was at the head table with about ten other men. We stood at the door until a waiter came and asked us what we wanted. I told him I wanted to speak to my father and pointed him out. I must say he looked a little amazed and it was no wonder as we must have been a sight. However, he went over and whispered in Daddy's ear. I guess alot of men would have been angry about being interrupted in the middle of such a meeting, but not our Daddy. We always came first with him. He just stood up and asked if he could have a few minutes to speak to his daughter. He seemed so glad to see us and asked if we had had breakfast. He told us that Mother was in town at Aunt Lydia's and gave me some money to have breakfast and then take a cab to her place. He said he would pick us up there later and take us home to Brandon.

Aunt Lydia was so happy to see us and said Mother had just gone to the store. She then insisted on hiding us in the coat closet to surprise Mother when she went to hang up her coat. It was so good to be back where people really cared about us again.

When we got back to Brandon and had dropped Marg off at her place I sat down with

Mother, Nona and Evelyn and told them the whole story. Mother said I should never have taken on such a thing, that there were other ways of handling that situation if we had only asked for help. Evelyn and Nona both said they might have been able to help if given the chance. The only thing I never told Mother was who the baby's father was. That would only have hurt her and the girls agreed that it was something she didn't have to know.

Mother thought that Marg's parents should know but I explained that Marg felt they would never forgive her. Mother said we hadn't given them much credit. But she agreed to keep our secret, as she said she was sure Marg would tell them in her own time. She also said she was proud of me for standing by my friend when she was in trouble.

It was great to be home after being away so long. Billy and Gerry had grown a lot and were so cute. They were the same size now and Evelyn dressed them alike, so they were always taken for twins. Gerry was the wild one and Billy was always a little more sober. Nona and I loved taking Billy out with us when we went downtown, but we found Gerry a handful as he would be into everything in the stores. Evelyn got a harness for him and we found that better as we could keep track of him easier.

Buddy and Ronnie were planning to go to the west coast on a job for a while with a fellow they had met who was working out there. The day they left we packed a big lunch for them, making sure we included several cans of port and beans for Ronnie, as he loved them. After they left it seemed so quiet in the house we could hardly stand it. However the quiet never lasted too long with Gerry around.

I had gotten a job at the Brandon college in the kitchen. It was only part time but the pay was not bad and I liked the work. My job was to fix the desserts on little plates for their lunch. It was a lot of work as there were a lot of students who ate there. After lunch I would collect the little plates and wash them and put them away. It took me about four hours.

Evelyn was not working yet and was finding it hard to get by since Buddy broke up the band. Without that money she really was not bringing in anything. One day at work I heard they were looking for another full time cook. When I got off after lunch I went into the dieticians office and told the dietician about Evelyn. I told her that Evelyn was a good cook. Of course I neglected to say she had never cooked anywhere but at home. Anyway, the dietician said to bring her over when I came to work the next day.

Daddy thought it was a real joke and couldn't stop laughing, but Evelyn surprised him by saying she was going to try for the job. She really did not think she would get it with no experience, but she needed a job badly so the next day she was ready to go. She was so nervous all the way over. She kept saying "you know they won't hire me". But somehow she must have fumbled through the interview, as she came out with the job. When she got home she got out all the cook books and tried to multiply the recipies to make them feed about two hundred people. Well to everyone's surprise she got along very well and found she really liked the work. She said she liked it far better than being a secretary and planned on making it her life's work. She was also making enough money to support herself and the boys.

Johnnie and his Mother were always wanting to come and see the boys, but Daddy said he was not to come to the house until he was helping to support them. One day after one of his long phone calls, she agreed to bring them down to his Mothers on the Sunday and he could see them there. He had never seen Gerry. When she got there he wasn't even home. She waited for a couple of hours as his Mother and sisters were really enjoying the visit and then finally brought them home. His mother was really angry with Evelyn, but she told her that since he wasn't working there was no reason why he wasn't there, that he obviously wasn't that interested.

This of course only made his Mother angrier. When Evelyn got home she said she would not make the effort again.

CHAPTER THIRTY NINE

Mother quit teaching school at the end of the term. She said she had taught long enough. She was now in her late fifties and had taught school since she was eighteen, with only about fifteen years off when she was in Alpine. She was not eligible for a pension as some of her years had been in Saskatchewan. At that time you had to do all your teaching in one province. It seemed unfair as Mother had been among the teachers who had first begun to fight for a teachers union. She had been fired from a school in Brandon for it. But that was how it was then. I know it is different now. You can teach anywhere in Canada and still get a pension when you are done.

Evelyn got the offer of a very good job with the Parks Board at Clear Lake. She had to stay there all week and came home for the weekends. However she was only there for three months and really missed the boys. Then one weekend she found the boys were shy of her and instead of going to her when they wanted anything they would come to Mother or Nona or I. So she quit and came home.

One night Mother and Daddy had a talk with her and they suggested that we take a trip out and see the boys and maybe Evelyn could work out there for awhile until Johnnie found someone else to bother. They said that she could leave Billy and Gerry with them until things settled down. It was desperate measures I thought, but Daddy went and got our tickets and away we went.

Mother packed lemon tarts, cakes and cookies, that Mrs. Southerland had made, in a box for us to take to the boys. We had a great time on the trip out and stopped over at Medicine Hat for a night. The fellows at the bus depot kept phoning us at the hotel telling us they were eating our tarts. And finally we went over there to make sure they were alright. After having a cup of coffee with them we left after making sure the boys baking was still there. The next morning we slept in and missed the bus so we had to stay another night.

When we got on the bus again we found it was going through the States and we thought that was just fine, as we had never been into the States. When the bus stopped at Coeur d' Alene in Idaho we found it such a lovely spot that we stayed over there for a night. We walked all over admiring the scenery. We always said we would like to go back some day, but never did.

When we finally got to the customs at Blaine Washington our pastry was getting pretty old looking and the customs officer said we could not take baked goods across the line. He wondered how we had got it into the States and we told him no one ever checked what we had. Anyway, Evelyn argued with him telling him our mother wanted us to bring this stuff to our brothers in White Rock. Finally the officer said "if your mother made this stuff and you've brought it all this way, far be it for me to stop it now". So we brought it all the way and showed it to the boys and then threw it out as it was all mouldy.

Now that was how we all began to migrate to B.C. We got jobs and married, Daddy retired and he and Mother and the children moved to B.C.

I will end this story of us now, as to go on would be a whole other book. Maybe I'll write it some day.

EPILOGUE

Ronnie was the only one of us who went back to Brandon and stayed there. He had gone back to work with Uncle Lloyd in the hatchery. There he met a woman who had tragically lost her husband. She had three children and was expecting her fourth when her husband was killed. Her name was Betty and she was working in a cafe to get by. Ronnie would go in for coffee and took a liking to her eight year old son. He seemed so lost and lonely. I guess he was missing his father so Ronnie would sit and talk to him and began taking him to ball games. Betty's mother was from Prince Edward Island, but had come to stay with Betty and look after the children until she got on her feet. I'm sure she wanted to go home, but was staying until an insurance policy was settled. A year after they met, they were married and had one daughter of their own. The five children all grew up and turned out very well.

Daddy died at seventy six and we were all at the hospital with him. The day before he died Evelyn and I were trying to lift him up on this pillows. We were having a hard time and Daddy kind of laughed and said "oh you bums". We treasured that moment as it was the last time he called us bums. Then he told us to look after

Mother and I'm proud to say we did. She had a room in all our houses and enjoyed going from one to the other. She died at ninety seven.

Nona married a postman from Calgary and lived there until she passed away of cancer. Her husband had gone before her, so when she became ill Evelyn and I spent four years taking turns going to Calgary to be with her.

Evelyn married a nice man from Revelstoke and lived there long after he passed on. When she became sick she came to live with me.

Buddy married a girl from close by and they had three children and after many years they divorced. He and his ex remained good friends but for some reason they could not live together. Buddy had a heart attack at sixty six and since his heart had stopped for some time he lost his short term memory and had to live in a home. He passed on at seventy after a short illness.

I married a wild Irishman and we lived on a hobby farm in Surrey, B.C. We had two children, a boy and a girl. He died after a fall at fifty six and I thank God for the time I had with him and for my wonderful children. They have been the best gift God has given me.

Sadly, Gerry died of an over dose of drugs at twenty seven. That was a heartbreak. He was a handsome loving young man and we all found it so hard to understand.

Fifty years after we left Alpine, Ronnie, Betty, Buddy, Evelyn and I went back to our cousin George's memorial service. He and his wife had lived in Vernon, B.C., but his wife wanted to have him buried in Alpine. She said he always called it home. Albert Josiphson was a minister in White Rock, B.C., but he went to Alpine and opened the old church for George's service. They only opened the church for special services now and for us it was really great to be there and see the place that had meant so much to us at one time. Strangely it had not changed all that much.

The old school where Mother had taught when she was so young, and where we had all gone to school had been turned into a community hall and that was where we had tea after the service.

We saw the house where we were born and to our surprise there it stood among waving trees. We were sorry we couldn't get right up to it as the road was gone, but seeing it from a distance was better than nothing.

Before we left for B.C., Ronnie took Joan, Evelyn, Buddy and I out to Bellafield. The school was gone and they had made a park in its place, as it had been one of the oldest schools in Manitoba. There was a large stone monument with all the names of the teachers who had taught there and the students who had attended school there. Mother and Aunt May's names were on both, as they had started school there as well as taught there. It was a great trip down memory lane and I must say writing this book has also brought back memories of a family who loved, laughed and cried together. As Nona's husband put it when he gave the toast to Les, Evelyn's husband, at their wedding. "Welcome to the family. I think you're going to like them".

Eileen Shannon

ABOUT THE AUTHOR

Eileen Shannon was born in Benito, Manitoba. The first ten years of her life was spent on a homestead in a small Swedish community called Alpine in the northern part of Manitoba. Her Mother had been a schoolteacher and when it became impossible to make a living on the farm in the 1930s she taught school in southern Manitoba. There the family lived in a small living quarters that was attached to the school for the duration of world war two while her Father worked at building Camp Shilo for training army personnel. They moved to a home in Brandon, Manitoba after the war and remained there, until they all moved to British Columbia.

www.ingramcontent.com/pod-product-compliance
Lightning Source LLC
Chambersburg PA
CBHW030312290526
45785CB00001B/329

9781403348135